EQUITY AND TRUSTS

Visit the *Law Express Series* Companion Website at **www.pearsoned.co.uk/lawexpress** to find valuable **student** learning material including:

- A study plan test to assess how well you know the subject before you begin your revision, now broken down into targeted study units
- Interactive quizzes with a variety of question types to test your knowledge of the main points from each chapter of the book
- Further examination questions and guidelines for answering them
- Interactive flashcards to help you revise the main terms and cases
- Printable versions of the topic maps and checklists

Plus:

- 'You be the marker' allows you to see exam questions and answers from the perspective of the examiner and includes notes on how an answer might be marked
- Podcasts provide point-by-poin exam question

LAW EXPRESS

Equity and Trusts

2nd edition

John Duddington
Worcester College of Technology

LawExpress

Harlow, England • London • New York • Boston • San Francisco • Toronto • Sydney • Singapore • Hong Kong
Tokyo • Seoul • Taipei • New Delhi • Cape Town • Madrid • Mexico City • Amsterdam • Munich • Paris • Milan

Pearson Education Limited
Edinburgh Gate
Harlow
Essex CM20 2JE
England

and Associated Companies throughout the world

Visit us on the World Wide Web at:
www.pearsoned.co.uk

First published 2007
Second edition published 2009

ISBN: 978-1-4058-7365-9

British Library Cataloguing-in-Publication Data
A catalogue record for this book is available from the British Library

Library of Congress Cataloging-in-Publication Data
Duddington, John.
Equity and trusts / John Duddington. – 2nd ed.
p. cm. – (Law express)
Includes bibliographical references and index.
ISBN 978-1-4058-7365-9 (alk. paper)
1. Equity–England–Outlines, syllabi, etc. 2. Equity–Wales–Outlines, syllabi, etc. 3. Trusts and trustees–England–Outlines, syllabi, etc. 4. Trusts and trustees–Wales–Outlines, syllabi, etc. I. title.
KD674.D83 2009
346.4205'9–dc22

2008024473

10 9 8 7 6 5 4 3 2 1
12 11 10 09 08

Typeset in 10pt Helvetica by 3
Printed and bound in Great Britain by Henry Ling Ltd, Dorchester, Dorset

The publisher's policy is to use paper manufactured from sustainable forests.

Contents

Supporting resources

Visit the *Law Express Series* Companion Website at **www.pearsoned.co.uk/lawexpress** to find valuable **student** learning material.

Companion Website for students

- A study plan test to assess how well you know the subject before you begin your revision, now broken down into targeted study units
- Interactive quizzes with a variety of question types to test your knowledge of the main points from each chapter of the book
- Further examination questions and guidelines for answering them
- Interactive flashcards to help you revise the main terms and cases
- Printable versions of the topic maps and checklists
- 'You be the marker' allows you to see exam questions and answers from the perspective of the examiner and includes notes on how an answer might be marked
- Podcasts provide point-by-point instruction on how to answer a common exam question

Also: The Companion Website provides the following features:

- Search tool to help locate specific items of content
- E-mail results and profile tools to send results of quizzes to instructors
- Online help and support to assist with website usage and troubleshooting

For more information please contact your local Pearson Education sales representative or visit **www.pearsoned.co.uk/lawexpress**

Dedication and acknowledgements

To my father, Walter Duddington, who first encouraged me to become a lawyer, and who would, I am sure, have been an equity enthusiast; to my wife Anne, for her constant support, loyalty and technical expertise without which my books would never begin to be written; to my daughter Mary, for her seemingly faultless proof reading and sense of fun which keeps me going; and to my son Christopher for just being himself. I would also like to thank my colleagues at Worcester Law School in the Property Law Team, Deborah Lister, Fiona ShawRoberts and Lesley Smallman, who have contributed more than they know!

Nor must I forget the staff of Pearson Education, especially Rebekah Taylor and Zoë Botterill, for their endless encouragement, cheerfulness and practical guidance, and the reviewers who sent in such detailed and helpful suggestions for this edition. I would have been delighted to have adopted more of these but for the limitations of space. However, I do hope that they see at least some of their ideas reflected in the pages of this book.

John Duddington
September 2008

Introduction

Most students achieve an average mark in equity exams, some do not pass at all and others do very well. So far, this is typical of all exams but in my experience the number of students who do very well is smaller then in other law exams. Why? This introduction aims to give you some pointers to getting into the category of those who do very well and equally pointers for simply achieving a pass.

REVISION NOTE

Success in exams in equity and trusts requires the following:

- An ability to tackle essay questions in such areas as the nature of equity, constructive trusts and equitable remedies.
- An ability to tackle complex problem questions in areas such as constitution of trusts, charities and secret trusts.

What are the problems which students commonly face in tackling these questions?

Essay questions

Equity is founded on a number of doctrines such as the concept of a fiduciary, unconscionability, notice and discretion in the grant of remedies. Students often simply scratch the surface when discussing these and this is the major reason why they do essay questions badly.

Take the concept of a fiduciary.

This is relevant in questions on constructive trusts, trustees, the nature of equity and undue influence. As such it is very well worth knowing some ideas of precisely what it means. But take a typical answer to this question:

> 'The concept of a fiduciary is at the heart of equity.' What do you understand by the term 'fiduciary' and to what extent is this true?

This appears to be relatively easy. Students can remember cases in which the fiduciary concept has been relevant and they put them together. I have read hundreds of answers like this. Cases such as *Boardman* v. *Phipps* (1967) and *A-G for Hong*

Kong v. *Reid* (1994) are dealt with and in each instance it is remarked that they are instances of the fiduciary principle. Possibly *Queensland Mines Ltd* v. *Hudson* is mentioned as an example of where the fiduciary principle did not apply.

This is leading to a mark of around 50 per cent. There is knowledge of the case law and students will be surprised that they have not done better in spite of all their work. The reason is simple: they have just scratched the surface. No attempt has been made to deal with the nature of the fiduciary concept. What is it about? A good answer would explain that the central idea is that of loyalty, which then translates into a principle that the fiduciary must not allow a conflict of interest between their duties as a fiduciary and their personal interests. How do fiduciary relationships arise? Is it through a voluntary undertaking on the part of the fiduciary? Moreover, the above examples of fiduciary relationships only refer to trustees. What about undue influence? Remember to take examples from as wide an area as possible. (Fiduciaries are mainly dealt with in Chapter 9 (for constructive trusts) and Chapter 2 (for undue influence). We will return to this question in the conclusion.

REVISION NOTE

The moral should be clear by now.
For answers to equity essay questions you must:

- Deal with theoretical concepts, usually at the start of your answer.
- Range widely.

A student intervenes at this point:

> How can I cover all the cases *and* deal with the theoretical issues?

Answer: you cannot so you will not be penalised for not doing so. Select a few cases, learn them well, read around them and relate them to the theoretical issues you have discussed. You will now be on the way to a good pass. *Less detail – more depth.*

Problem questions

These are easier as the structure of the problem gives you the structure of your answer. However, in equity problems there are often rather subtle points which, when picked up, can give you extra marks. A good example is secret and half-secret trusts (see Chapter 7), a very common area for problems.

Here is one example:

> The generally accepted rule for communication of a half-secret trust is that the details of the trust must be communicated before the will (*Re Keen* (1937)). However, *Re Keen* is also authority for another rule which can conflict with this:

that the details must be communicated in accordance with the terms of the will. Again an answer which scores about 50 per cent will mention and apply the first rule, which is probably the correct one. However, an answer which also applies the other rule will clearly score more. (These rules are all dealt with in Chapter 7.) Another subtle point arising here is the law where the trust is communicated to one trustee but not the other. Is the one to whom it is not communicated bound? (See *Re Stead* (1900)). Learn these rather tricky points thoroughly! Constitution of trusts is another area with many a subtlety!

About this book

This book is not a potted version of the subject. You will not find in it all the detail which you need to pass your exams. It is an aid to learning and not a substitute to reading textbooks, articles (essential if you want a good pass) and of course attendance at lectures, tutorials and seminars. It can be used either at the end of the course as a revision aid or during the course to guide you along.

Guided tour

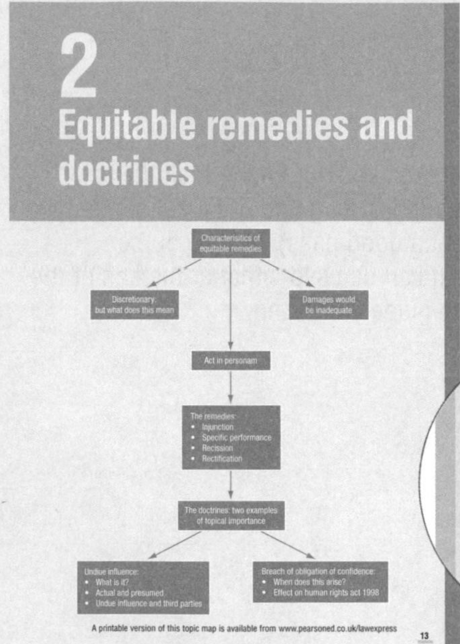

Topic maps – Highlight the main points and allow you to find your way quickly and easily through each chapter.

Revision checklist – How well do you know each topic? Don't panic if you don't know them all, the chapters will help you to revise each point so that you will be fully prepared for your exams.

QUITABLE REMEDIES AN

Revision Checklist

Essential points you should

- [ ] the characteristics of equitable rem
- [ ] the situations in which a grant of th performance, rescission and rectific
- [ ] the meaning of undue influence
- [ ] the situations when undue influen
- [ ] the effect of undue influence (ap
- [ ] the situations when an obliga

Sample questions – Prepare for what you will be faced with in your exams! Guidance on structuring strong answers is provided at the end of the chapter.

Sample questions

Could you answer this question? Below is a typical essay question that could arise on this topic. Guidelines on answering the question are included at the end of this chapter, whilst a sample problem question and guidance on tackling it can be found on the companion website.

Essay question

'Equitable remedies are discretionary.'

Do you agree?

Key definition boxes – Make sure you understand essential legal terms.

KEY DEFINITION

An **injunction** is a court order requiring a party either to do or not to do a particular act.

An **injunction** may be used:

- to restrain a breach of contract
- to restrain the commission of a tort (e.g. a nuisance or a trespass)
- to restrain a breach of confidence
- to restrain a breach of trust
- in matrimonial and family matters. (The Family Law Act 1996 gives the courts extensive powers to grant injunctions in divorce proceedings.)

Problem area boxes – Highlight areas where students most often trip up in exams. Use them to make sure you do not make the same mistakes.

PROBLEM AREA: injunctions and SP

Some cases appear to deal with injunctions and not SP even though they appear in textbooks under the heading of SP. This is because there is an overlap:

- SP: you must carry out the contract.
- Injunction: you must not fail to carry out the contract.

Key case and key statute boxes – Identify the essential cases and statutes that you need to know for your exams.

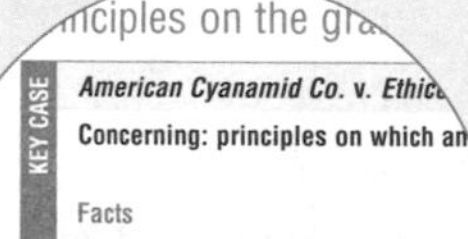

KEY STATUTE

Trade Union and Labour Relations Act 1992, s.236

This prohibits the courts from enforcing performance of cc employment either by specific performance or injunction . actual contracts of employment, not to other contracts of |

Further thinking boxes – Illustrate areas of academic debate, and point you towards that extra reading required for the top grades.

FURTHER THINKING

These orders were criticised on the ground that they could allow oppressive conduct, amounting to the ransacking of a business, when there was no case proved against that person. See Dockray and Laddie (1990) and, for a case example, *Lock International plc* v. *Beswick* (1989).

In *Universal Thermosensors* v. *Hibben* (1992) conditions were imposed on the use of these search orders which have now been incorporated into the standard form (see also Practice Direction Civil Practice Rules 25 para.7).

Glossary – Forgotten the meaning of a word? – Where a word is highlighted in the text, turn to the glossary at the back of the book to remind yourself of its meaning.

Glossary

Key definitions

Advancement	Payment of capital to beneficiaries before they are entitled.
Bare trustee	A trustee with no active duties and so can be given directions by the beneficiary to transfer the legal estate.
Benificiaries	Those for whom the property is held in trust.
Constitution of a trust	A trust is constituted when the legal title to the trust property is vested in the trustee(s).
Constructive trusts	Defined by Millett (Equity's Place in the Law of Commerce 1998 114 LQR 214) as arising 'whenever the circumstances are such that it would be unconscionable for the owner of the legal title to assert his own beneficial interest and deny the beneficial interest of another'.

Exam tips – Want to impress examiners? These indicate how you can improve your exam performance and your chances of getting top marks.

EXAM TIP

You may feel that rather a lot of attention has been given to interlocutory injunctions but they do come up quite a bit in exams. In addition the two special types of injunctions set out below are interlocutory.

Revision notes – Highlight points that you should be aware of in other topic areas, or where your course may adopt a specific approach that you should check with your course tutor before reading further.

REVISION NOTE

Go back to Chapter 1 and check that you are familiar with this case. It is an excellent illustration of equitable remedies.

In *Patel* v. *Ali* (1984) you can see that:

- Equitable remedies, although discretionary, are not granted at the whim of the court: note the phrase 'hardship amounting to injustice' as the principle here.

Guided tour of the companion website

Book resources are available to download. Print your own **topic maps** and **revision checklists!**

Use the **study plan** prior to your revision to help you assess how well you know the subject and determine which areas need most attention. Choose to take the full assessment or focus on targeted study units.

'Test your knowledge' of individual areas with quizzes tailored specifically to each chapter. A variety of multiple choice, true and false and fill-in-the-blank question types ensure you are prepared for anything. Sample problem and essay questions are also available with guidance on crafting a good answer.

Flashcards help improve recall of important legal terms and key cases. Use online, print for a handy reference or download to iPod for on-the-go revision!

'You be the marker' gives you the chance to evaluate sample exam answers for different question types and understand how and why an examiner awards marks.

Download the **podcast** and listen as your own personal Law Express tutor guides you through a 10-15 minute audio session. You will be presented with a typical but challenging question and provided a step-by-step explanation on how to approach the question, what essential elements your answer will need for a pass, how to structure a good response, and what to do to make your answer stand out so that you can earn extra marks.

All of this and more can be found when you visit **www.pearsoned.co.uk/lawexpress**

Table of cases and statutes

Cases

Abbot v. *Abbott* (2007) WL 2126561 **110, 123**

A-G for Hong Kong v. *Reid* [1994] AC 324 HL **ix, 121, 172**

A-G v. *Guardian Newspapers Ltd* (No. 2) [1988] 3 All ER 545 HL **27**

Allen v. *Distillers Co. (Biochemicals) Ltd* [1974] QB 384 **162**

American Cyanamid Co. v. *Ethicon Ltd* [1975] 2 WLR 396 HL **17**

Anthony v. *Donges* (1998) 2 FLR 775 HC **36**

Anton Piller KG v. *Manufacturing Processes Ltd* [1976] Ch 55 **18**

Armitage v. *Nurse* [1998] Ch 221 HC **155**

Australian Securities and Investments Commission v. *Citigroup Global Markets Australia Pty Ltd* (2007) FCA 963 **155**

Barclays Bank Ltd v. *Quistclose Investments Ltd* [1970] AC 567 HL **7, 112**

Barclays Bank plc v. *O'Brien* [1994] 1 AC 180 **14, 25**

Barlow Clowes International Ltd (in liquidation) v. *Vaughan* [1992] 4 All ER 22 **180**

Barlow Clowes International Ltd (in liquidation) v. *Eurotrust International Ltd* (2006) 1 WLR 1476 **177**

Bank of Credit and Commerce International (Overseas) Ltd (in liquidation) v. *Akindele* [2001] Ch 437 **176**

Binions v. *Evans* [1972] Ch 359 **117, 124**

Bishopsgate Investment Management (in liquidation) v. *Homan* [1995] Ch 211 CA **178**

Blackwell v. *Blackwell* [1929] AC 318 **95, 96**

Boardman v. *Phipps* [1967] 2 AC 46 HL **ix, 118, 120, 124, 146, 147, 175**

Bray v. *Ford* [1896] AC 44 **149**

Burns v. *Burns* [1984] 1 All ER 244 **123**

Cannon v. *Hartley* [1949] Ch 213 **82**

Carl Zeiss Siftung v. *Herbert Smith & Co. (a firm) (No. 2)* [1969] 2 Ch 276 **119**

Carly v. *Farrelly* (1975) 1 NZLR 356 **124**

Carreras Rothmans Ltd v. *Freeman Matthews Treasure Ltd* (1985) Ch 207 **113**

Chapman v. *Chapman* [1954] AC 429 **162**

Chichester Diocesan Fund and Board of Finance Inc. v. *Simpson* [1944] AC 341 HL **140**

Statutes

1 Nature of equity and trusts

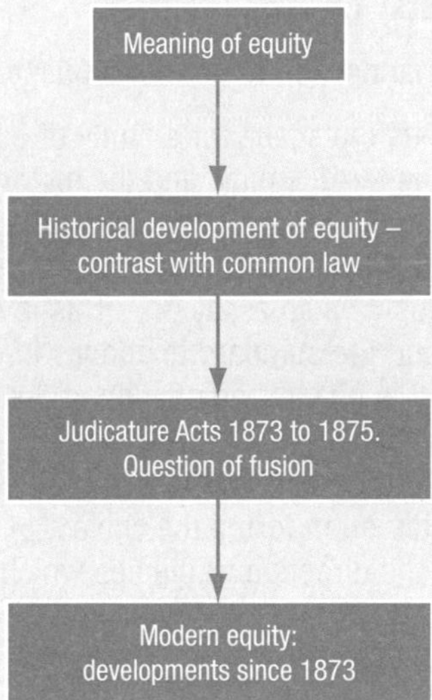

A printable version of this topic map is available from www.pearsoned.co.uk/lawexpress

Revision Checklist

Essential points you should know:

- [ ] the meanings of the term equity
- [ ] the reasons why equity developed as a separate system of law
- [ ] what is meant by the concept of a trust
- [ ] the later development of equity in outline
- [ ] the modern arguments for and against whether equity and the common law are now fused.

Introduction: **Understanding equity**

This chapter is perhaps the most important in this book.

However, unlike all others chapters, it:

- does not contain all the material needed to answer a question.

The reason is that this chapter sets the scene for a study of equity and, in addition to guiding you on the meaning of the term 'equity' and the history of its development, it points you in the direction of various themes in the study of equity. The detail on some of these will be found in later chapters. A question on the nature and/or development of equity will obviously be an essay one. This is one area where it is absolutely essential to read beyond the standard textbooks in order to gain an above average pass on a question and this chapter points you in the direction of a variety of additional reading in the 'Further thinking' sections.

It also has a separate section on the development of the trust and the uses to which trusts can be put today. This often forms the subject of an exam question and, again, this section points you in the direction of themes which are picked up in more depth in later chapters.

Assessment advice

Essay questions

An essay question can take one of these forms:

1 The historical development of equity. This would be less likely than the other possibilities.
2 The relationship between equity and the common law. This is the most likely area, as it will involve you in looking at the distinctive features of equity and contrasting them with the common law. There is the opportunity to use your knowledge of other areas (e.g. contract and tort) when you discuss the common law and this will gain added marks.
3 The possibility of equity and the common law converging in the future. This is an area on which a good deal has been written recently and so you need to have read widely in order to be able to answer it well. On the whole it is not dealt with in much depth in the standard textbooks.
4 The uses to which trusts can be put with an emphasis on their versatility.

Two other points:

1 It is possible for a question to cover all of these issues, for example, it may ask you to analyse the reasons why equity developed, how significant it is today and how it may develop in future.
2 Be careful to check if the question asks you to discuss 'modern equity'. Modern really means since the Judicature Acts and so no credit will be given for historical material here. It is a common error among students to feel that they must include historical material whatever the question says. Resist it!

Sample question

Could you answer this question? Below is a typical essay question that could arise on this topic. Guidelines on answering the question are included at the end of this chapter, whilst another sample essay question and guidance on tackling it can be found on the companion website.

Essay question

'The courts in their equitable jurisdiction have more scope for developing the law in a conscionable manner than they have in their common law jurisdiction.'

(Hayton and Marshall, 2005)

Evaluate this statement by reference to the growth and development of modern equity.

Meaning of equity

Equity has various meanings:

In a general sense equity means fairness or justice. However, this is too general on its own for law exams and also it takes us into a wider debate about what precisely 'fairness' and 'justice' mean. Instead we need to:

- consider the term 'conscience': this has a long history in equity – the Chancellor was known as the Keeper of the King's Conscience
- consider recent cases where the courts have used the term 'unconscionability' which at least is derived from conscience (e.g. see *Pennington* v. *Waine* (2002) in Chapter 6)
- make it clear that equity today does not mean the same as justice in the broad sense
- state the principle that equity may intervene where the application of a strict rule of law would cause injustice (e.g. it might allow a mortgage to be redeemed even though the actual redemption date had passed)
- state that in the legal sense equity means the body of principles developed by the Court of Chancery.

In an essay on the nature of equity you could then move on to look at characteristics of equity: it is discretionary, it acts as a supplement to the common law (not a complete system on its own), it acts *in personam*, etc.

For all these points you need examples drawn from equity and this is a good opportunity to show your wide knowledge.

KEY CASE

***Patel* v. *Ali* (1984) Ch. 283 (HC)**

Concerning: principles for the grant of an equitable remedy

Facts

A contract was made for the sale of a house but during a long delay in going on to completion the seller had a leg amputated and she gave birth to her second and third children. This meant that she came to rely on help from friends and relatives. The buyers sought specific performance (SP) (equitable remedy) to compel the seller to complete.

Legal principle

SP would be refused as there would be hardship amounting to injustice if it was granted because the seller would lose the help on which she relied if she was forced to move.

Note: This is an excellent case to build part of an answer on the nature of equity round. It shows:

- Equitable remedies are discretionary – common law ones are not. She would have to pay damages (common law remedy) for her breach of the contract of sale.
- Equity is not just a question of the court exercising a complete discretion: there are certain principles on which it exercises a discretion. In the above case the court emphasised that to compel the seller to move would amount to 'hardship amounting to injustice'. The normal rule is that SP is granted in contracts for the sale of land where the seller fails to complete; in this case the rule was displaced. An exam question often asks if equity is just a matter of the court in each case having a complete discretion. Here is part of your answer, although you will need to say that some judges do give the impression that equity is just individual discretion on their part – see below.

FURTHER THINKING

You should research the term 'unconscionability'. Take this quote from Duddington (2006: 18): 'unconscionability is valuable as a general pointer to the direction to which equity should take, but it is of no use as a practical tool in the application of equitable principles, for, in the end, principle is what equity is about.' Note the mention of equity being based on principle and link this to the discussion of discretion in equity below. Read Hopkins (2006) who considers the utility of unconscionability as a rationale for equitable intervention.

Figure 1.1 gives you a historical context.

Figure 1.1

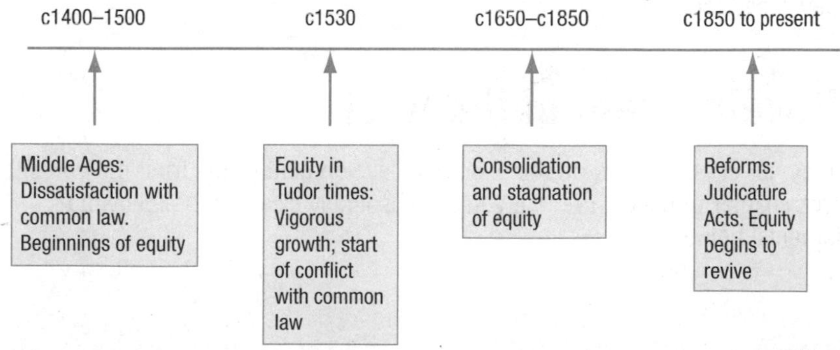

Exam questions are not likely to ask you just for an historical account of equity and so you should look at the history to see if it gives pointers to how equity operates today, which is a much more likely area for a question.

Maxims of equity

These are signposts to how equitable jurisdiction might be exercised but are not fixed rules. Examples, with where illustrations on their application may be found in this book, are:

- Equity looks to the intent and not the form (Chapters 6 and 7).
- Equity will not allow a statute to be used as an instrument of fraud (Chapters 7 and 9).
- Equity will not assist a volunteer (Chapter 4).

Look at how equity developed as a supplement to the common law (e.g. by using remedies such as injunctions and SP to prevent injustice and then mention that this is still the case today (e.g. the modern *Mareva* (freezing) and *Anton Piller* (search) orders which are examples of injunctions (see Chapter 2).

Look at how equity gradually developed maxims and then give examples of how these are still used today.

FURTHER THINKING

Tinsley v. *Milligan* (1994) is an excellent example of how the Court of Appeal and the House of Lords both used the maxim 'he who comes to equity must come with clean hands' but applied it differently (see Chapter 8).

You should also look at how trusts were originally used and at how the trust concept has developed today.

Development of the trust

You may not get questions on the historical development of the trust but you should use this chapter to make sure that you are absolutely clear on the following fundamental points:

What is a trust?

KEY DEFINITION

'A **trust** is a relationship which arises when property is vested in a person (or persons) called the trustees, which those trustees are obliged to hold for the benefit of other persons called the cestuis que trust or beneficiaries' (Hanbury and Martin (2005): 47).

Who is the settlor?

KEY DEFINITION

The **settlor** is in effect the creator of the trust which is created by the settlor transferring property to the trustees to hold on trust or alternatively declaring that they are the trustees. If the trust is created by will then the trust is created by the testator.

Who are the beneficiaries?

KEY DEFINITION

The **beneficiaries** are those for whom the property is held on trust and therefore they have the equitable interest in the property.

The idea that the **beneficiaries** have an equitable interest in the **trust** property is one of the concepts at the heart of equity. It underlies cases such as *Barclays Bank* v. *Quistclose Investments Ltd* (1970) (see Chapter 8). The effect is that in equity the beneficiaries own the trust property and so if it is wrongly taken from the trust they are not just in the position of creditors who have to claim the return of money owed to them as a debt. Instead the beneficiaries may be able to use the remedies set out in Chapter 13.

Suppose that someone has purchased the trust property. Can the beneficiaries reclaim it from them? This brings us to another definition.

KEY DEFINITION

A purchaser is taken to have **notice** of an equitable interest unless they had either actual notice of the equitable interest of the beneficiaries, or constructive notice or imputed notice.

- Actual **notice** means actual knowledge.
- Constructive notice means that the purchaser should have been aware of the equitable interest had reasonable enquires been made.
- Imputed notice means that if the agent or employee of the purchaser had notice then the purchaser will also have notice.

REVISION NOTE

If you are studying land law or have studied it then go back to your land law materials and check what it says on notice. See *Land Law* in the Law Express Series, especially Chapters 1 and 2.

Judicature Acts 1873 and 1875 and the question of fusion

The Judicature Acts abolished both the old common law courts and the Court of Chancery and replaced them with a new Supreme Court consisting of the High Court and the Court of Appeal. The Judicature Act 1873 provided that where equity and the common law conflict then equity shall prevail (s.25(11)). The passage of this Act led to a debate which is still not settled on the extent to which equity and the common law are fused.

The question of whether equity and the common law are fused or not is a very familiar area for exam questions. It is an issue which is still debated and so there is no right answer – do not feel that you have to come to one!

Fusion can mean two things:

1 That the *administration* of equity and the common law is fused. This is so as all divisions of the High Court have jurisdiction in both common law and equity unlike before when only the Court of Chancery exercised equitable jurisdiction.
2 That the actual systems of common law and equity have been fused so that it is no longer correct to speak of common law and equity but of one system. This aspect has given rise to debate. Lord Diplock in *United Scientific Holdings* v. *Burnley BC* [1978] considered that law and equity are fused, in contrast to the well-known statement of Ashburner in *Principles of Equity* (1933) who compared law and equity to separate streams which although running side by side 'do not mingle their waters'. In fact there has been a vigorous growth in equity since the middle years of the twentieth century. See, for example, the fiduciary concept (Chapter 9) the law on trusts of the home (Chapter 9) and equitable doctrines and remedies (Chapter 2).

EXAM TIP

When reading this book, make a note of the areas where equity's intervention has been more marked as indicated above as this could form the basis of an answer on equity. Try to include examples from as wide a range as possible This is dealt with in more detail below.

The question of fusion is somewhat out of date now and exam questions may instead ask you if law and equity ought to exist as separate systems of law at all.

FURTHER THINKING

The debate on the future of equity as a separate system and if it is necessary to regard equitable and common law jurisdiction as distinct is current at the moment and you must be aware of it for the exam. Sarah Worthington in her book *Equity* (2006) argues strongly for the end of two distinct systems. She points out that the origin of equity is to be found in history and not policy. This is unarguable but it is easy to forget that it is so. For a view that trusts do not need to exist under a system of equitable duties and rights see Honore (2003).

What is clear is that the Judicature Acts did fuse the administration of law and equity.

KEY CASE

***Walsh* v. *Lonsdale* (1882) 21 Ch D 9 (HC)**

Concerning: effect of the Judicature Acts

Facts

A lease was granted but not by deed. Thus it was only equitable – an agreement for a lease can be enforced by equity on the basis of the maxim that 'equity looks on that as done which ought to be done', i.e. if a person has agreed to grant a lease then they ought to do so and, as far as possible, equity will assume that they have done so.

Legal principle

The Court applied s.25(ii) of the Judicature Act 1873 and held that, as equity prevailed, there was an equitable lease..

Modern equity – developments since 1875

This is a likely area for exam questions and you will find the following chapters particularly useful:

- Chapter 2: Equitable remedies and doctrines
- Chapters 8 and 9: Resulting trusts and Constructive trusts – especially thinking about how the constructive trust can be used
- Chapter 9: the section on Trusts of the home – the extent to which equity has recognised rights here has been one of the best modern examples of equity.

Note also the following:

- the extent to which equity is flourishing in Australia (e.g see. *Queensland Mines Ltd* v. *Hudson* (1978) in Chapter 9
- in various cases judges are starting to base their decisions on wider grounds (e.g. unconscionability) see, for example, *Pennington* v. *Waine* (2002) in Chapter 6
- how judges often today seem more forward looking than, for example, judges in the 1950s (e.g. see the judgments of Lord Simonds in a number of charity cases in Chapter 10 such as *Oppenheim* v. *Tobacco Securities Trust Co. Ltd* and *Gilmour* v. *Coates*).
- the variety of uses to which trusts are put – this is dealt with more fully in one of the model answers on the companion website.

Chapter summary: **Putting it all together**

TEST YOURSEL F

- ☐ Can you tick all the points from the **revision checklist** at the beginning of this chapter?
- ☐ Take the **end-of-chapter quiz** on the companion website.
- ☐ Test your knowledge of the cases with the **revision flashcards** on the website.
- ☐ Attempt the **essay question** from the beginning of this chapter using the guidelines below.
- ☐ Go to the companion website to try out **other questions**.

Answer guidelines

See the essay question at the start of the chapter.

You need to select no more than four areas and look at the contribution of equity. Never make the mistake of trying to say something about everything: you will end up by not saying anything worth saying about anything!

Take, for example, trusts of the family home. How did equity intervene? What did it do that the common law could not have done?

Continue this approach with other areas, for example, secret trusts and constructive trusts.

Make your answer stand out

End by referring to the debate about the place of equity – although it may have made a great contribution in the past is there a need for it today? Does the common law recognise issues of conscience? Is it capable of doing so?

FURTHER READING

Ashburner, W. (1933) *Principles of Equity*, 2nd edn, London: Butterworths.

Duddington, J. (2006) *Essentials of Equity and Trusts*, Harlow: Pearson Education.

Hanbury and Martin, J. (2005) *Modern Equity*, 17th edn, London: Sweet and Maxwell.

Hayton, D. and Marshall, O. (2005) *The Law of Trusts and Equitable Remedies*, 17th edn, London: Sweet and Maxwell.

Honore, T. (2003) 'Trusts, the Inessentials' in *Rationalizing Property, Equity and Trusts: Essays in Honour of Edward Burn*, ed. Getzler, J., London: Lexis Nexis.
Hopkins, N. (2006) 'Conscience, discretion and the creation of property rights', 26 LS 475.
Mason, A. 'The Place of Equity and Equitable Remedies in the Common Law World', 110 LQR 238.
Worthington, S. (2006) *Equity*, 2nd edn, Oxford: Oxford University Press.

2 Equitable remedies and doctrines

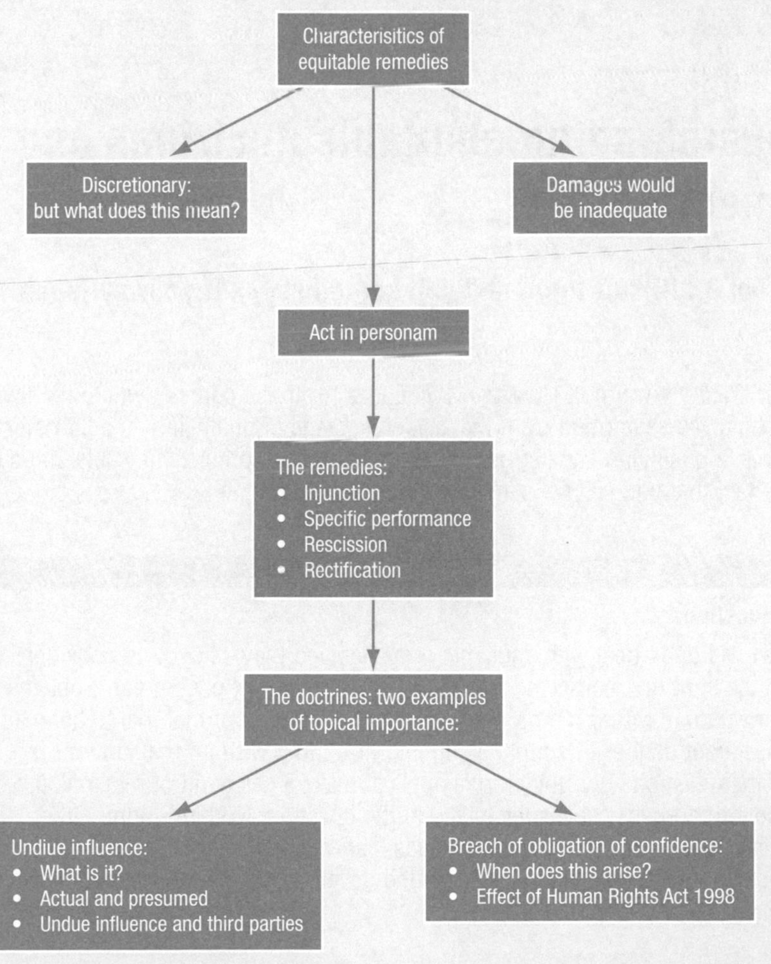

A printable version of this topic map is available from www.pearsoned.co.uk/lawexpress

Revision Checklist

Essential points you should know:

- [ ] the characteristics of equitable remedies
- [ ] the situations in which a grant of the remedies of injunction, specific performance, rescission and rectification would be appropriate
- [ ] the meaning of undue influence
- [ ] the situations when undue influence is presumed and when it is not
- [ ] the effect of undue influence (and misrepresentation) on third parties
- [ ] the situations when an obligation of confidence may be imposed.

Introduction: Understanding equitable doctrines and remedies

This is not a difficult topic and you should check if your syllabus includes it.

If it is just 'trusts' it will not. However, syllabuses for those courses where the final qualification gives exemption from the academic stage of qualifying as a barrister or solicitor (i.e. a qualifying law degree) must include equity other than trusts and so it is almost certain that you will be examined on equity as such.

Assessment advice

Essay questions

An essay will often deal with equitable remedies and may ask you to consider them in the light of a particular quotation. This should not pose great problems of understanding; rather the problem is often the amount of material to hand and the consequent danger of simply ploughing through it with no real attempt to answer the question. The golden rule applies: make a selection of material and then use it to address the issues raised in the question. Nothing more! Other possibilities are essays on undue influence, especially the decision in *Barclays Bank* v. *O'Brien* (1994), and on the developing case law on breach of confidence.

Assessment advice

Problem questions

Problem questions are less likely on the remedies although possible ones could be on specific performance, freezing and/or search orders.

A more likely area is undue influence where there are various issues to explore and this is the area chosen for a problem question on the companion website to this chapter.

Sample question

Could you answer this question? Below is a typical essay question that could arise on this topic. Guidelines on answering the question are included at the end of this chapter, whilst a sample problem question and guidance on tackling it can be found on the companion website.

Essay question

'Equitable remedies are discretionary.'

Do you agree?

Characteristics of equitable remedies

1 **They are discretionary,** whereas the common law remedy of damages is available as of right. This does not, however, mean that everything is left to the discretion of the court in each case: as we shall see, there are clear principles governing the grant of equitable remedies.
2 **They are granted where the common law remedies (e.g. damages) would be inadequate** or where the common law remedies are not available because the right is exclusively equitable (e.g. a right of a beneficiary under a trust).
3 **They act *in personam*,** i.e. against the defendant personally.

Points (1) and (2) are illustrated by the case of *Patel* v. *Ali* [1984].

REVISION NOTE

Go back to Chapter 1 and check that you are familiar with this case. It is an excellent illustration of equitable remedies.

In *Patel* v. *Ali* (1984) you can see that:

- Equitable remedies, although discretionary, are not granted at the whim of the court: note the phrase 'hardship amounting to injustice' as the principle here.

- Damages could be granted to compensate the buyer.

The next section will look at the main remedies.

Injunctions

KEY DEFINITION

An **injunction** is a court order requiring a party either to do or not to do a particular act.

An **injunction** may be used:

- to restrain a breach of contract
- to restrain the commission of a tort (e.g. a nuisance or a trespass)
- to restrain a breach of confidence
- to restrain a breach of trust
- in matrimonial and family matters. (The Family Law Act 1996 gives the courts extensive powers to grant injunctions in divorce proceedings.)

Perpetual injunctions

Perpetual injunctions will not necessarily last forever but they are final in that they will finally resolve the issue between the parties. There are two types of perpetual injunction:

1. **Prohibitory**, i.e. restraining the doing of an act.
2. **Mandatory**, i.e. commanding the doing of an act.

Interlocutory injunctions

The object of an interlocutory injunction is to preserve the status quo until the trial of an action, for example, to restrain an association from holding a meeting without allowing certain members to attend (*Woodford* v. *Smith* (1970)).

They may be:

- prohibitory (see above)
- mandatory (see above), or
- *Quia timet.*

A *quia timet* injunction is granted to restrain a threatened apprehended injury to the claimant's rights even though no injury has yet occurred. For example, in *Torquay Hotel Co. Ltd.* v. *Cousins* (1969) the defendants, members of a trade union, intended to picket the claimant's hotel to prevent the delivery of fuel oil that would interfere with the execution of contracts which the claimants had made for the supply of fuel oil. A *quia timet* injunction was granted.

Interlocutory injunctions are often granted without notice to the other side – the old term for this was *ex parte*.

Principles on the grant of interlocutory injunctions

KEY CASE

***American Cyanamid Co.* v. *Ethicon Ltd.* [1975] AC 396 (HL)**

Concerning: principles on which an interlocutory injunction will be granted

Facts

There was an application for a *quia timet* injunction to prevent the infringement of a patent.

Legal principles

The court laid down the following principles to be followed when deciding to grant an interlocutory injunction:

(a) Is there a serious question to be tried? If the defendant has no arguable defence at all then an injunction will be granted and points (b) and (c) below do not arise. Otherwise the court will consider the following points:

(b) If there is a serious issue, will damages be an adequate remedy so that an injunction will not be needed? This must be looked at from the point of view of:
   (i) The claimant, i.e. would damages be adequate compensation for loss caused to him by acts of the defendant before the trial?
   (ii) The defendant, i.e. if the claimant loses at the trial then could any loss to the defendant be compensated by the claimant giving an undertaking in damages?

(c) If damages would be inadequate, then should an injunction be granted taking into account the balance of convenience to each party? *Hubbard* v. *Pitt* (1976) illustrates both (b) and (c).

(d) There may be other special factors to be considered as in the *American Cyanamid* case itself, where an interlocutory injunction was granted to prevent infringement of a patent for a pharmaceutical product and partly because of the argument that if the defendant's product had been used prior to the trial, and the claimant then obtained a permanent injunction against its further marketing, the claimant would themselves lose goodwill. Accordingly the interlocutory injunction prevented the defendants from marketing the product at all.

EXAM TIP

You may feel that rather a lot of attention has been given to interlocutory injunctions but they do come up quite a bit in exams. In addition the two special types of injunctions set out below are interlocutory.

Freezing order

This is an interlocutory injunction designed to prevent the defendant from disposing of assets which would otherwise be available to meet the claimant's claim or removing them from the courts' jurisdiction. The order is often known as a *Mareva* order from the decision in *Mareva Compania Naviera SA* v. *International Bulkcarriers SA* [1980].

The general principles laid down in the *American Cyanimid* case apply to when this remedy will be granted. Also, the claimant should:

- Have a good arguable case.
- Make full and frank disclosure of all material matters together with full particulars of his claim and its amount and should state fairly the points made against it by the defendant.
- Normally give grounds for believing that the defendants have assets in the jurisdiction. All assets are within the scope of a freezing order which has thus been ordered in relation to, for example, bank accounts (the most frequent situation), motor vehicles, jewellery and goodwill.
- Normally give grounds for believing either that the assets will be removed from the jurisdiction before the claim is satisfied or that in some way they might be dissipated.

Search order

These allow search of premises of a possible defendant and are especially useful where a defendant might destroy evidence once a claim form was served on him. They are used, for example, in cases of alleged video pirating.

In *Anton Piller KG* v. *Manufacturing Processes Ltd* (1976), Omrod LJ laid down the following conditions which must be satisfied by the claimant for the grant of the order:

- an extremely strong prima facie case
- actual or potential damage of a very serious nature
- clear evidence that the defendant has incriminating documents or things and a real possibility of their destruction before an application without notice can be made.

FURTHER THINKING

These orders were criticised on the ground that they could allow oppressive conduct, amounting to the ransacking of a business, when there was no case proved against that person. See Dockray and Laddie (1990) and, for a case example, *Lock International plc* v. *Beswick* (1989).

In *Universal Thermosensors* v. *Hibben* (1992) conditions were imposed on the use of these search orders which have now been incorporated into the standard form (see also Practice Direction Civil Practice Rules 25 para.7).

EXAM TIP

Freezing, and especially search orders, are an area where there is room for debate about the need to consider the interests of the party seeking the order and the party against whom it is being sought. Think about this issue for an essay question.

Specific performance

KEY DEFINITION

Specific performance (SP) is an order requiring the performance of obligations under a contract. Whereas injunctions are generally negative (you must not) SP is positive (you must).

EXAM TIP

Exam questions are likely to focus on the circumstances when an order of **specific performance (SP)** may be granted so look in detail at pairs of slightly contrasting cases and read round them to see if you can discover any principle. Do not learn masses of cases superficially but those you learn, learn well!

Problem area: Injunctions and SP

Some cases appear to deal with injunctions and not SP even though they appear in textbooks under the heading of SP. This is because there is an overlap:

- SP: you must carry out the contract.
- Injunction: you must not fail to carry out the contract.

Therefore in an exam question on SP you will gain extra marks for bringing in cases involving injunctions which illustrate this overlap.

The fundamental principle is that SP will not *normally* be granted in certain situations.

EXAM TIP

Note the use of the word 'normally' in the above sentence. Remember that equity is a discretionary system and so there are fewer black and white rules than in other areas of the law.

These are:

- Where damages would be an adequate remedy.

KEY CASE

***Sky Petroleum* v. *VIP Petroleum* [1974] 1 WLR 576**

Concerning: grant of an injunction, which would amount to specific performance, where damages would not be an adequate remedy

Facts

During a petrol shortage the defendants terminated their contract with the claimants to supply them with petrol.

Legal principle

An injunction was granted restraining the defendants from withholding supplies of petrol. There was a petrol shortage at the time and so, if only damages had been awarded to the claimants, they would have been unlikely to obtain supplies elsewhere..

- Where constant supervision would be needed by the court.

KEY CASE

***Co-operative Insurance Society* v. *Argyll Stores (Holdings) Ltd* [1998] AC 1 (HL)**

Concerning: principles to be applied when granting specific performance.

Facts

Specific performance was sought of an undertaking to keep a supermarket open during the usual hours of business in a lease which had still 19 years to run. The supermarket was an 'anchor store' in a shopping centre and its closure would badly affect the viability of the rest of the centre.

KEY CASE

Legal principle

The House of Lords considered that if the store was ordered to be kept open the loss to the tenant would exceed that which would be suffered by the landlord if the supermarket closed. In addition, the principle that the court would need to supervise any order of SP remained important.

FURTHER THINKING

This decision was regarded as a setback by those who favour an extension of this remedy (e.g. see Phang (1998).

- Where the contract is for personal services.

KEY STATUTE

Trade Union and Labour Relations Act 1992, s.236

This prohibits the courts from enforcing performance of contracts of employment either by specific performance or injunction. This only applies to actual contracts of employment, not to other contracts of personal service.

KEY CASE

***Page One Records* v. *Britton (t/a The Troggs)* [1967] 3 All ER 822 (HC)**

Concerning: use of an injunction in contracts of personal service

Facts

The claimant had been dismissed as manager of 'The Troggs' pop group and sought an injunction to restrain the group from engaging anyone else as manager.

Legal principle

This was refused as its effect would be to compel the defendant to continue to employ the claimant because it would need **a** manager.

KEY CASE

***Warner Bros Pictures Inc.* v. *Nelson* [1937] 1 KB 209 (HC)**

Concerning: use of an injunction in contracts of personal service

Facts

The actress (Bette Davis) agreed not to work as an actress for another film company for the period of her contract with Warner Bros.

Legal principle

The injunction would be granted on the ground that Miss Davis could earn a living doing other work. It would not force her to work for Warner Bros.

You should also consider *Warren* v. *Mendy* (1989).

There have been instances where the courts have enforced a contract for personal services against an employer, i.e. where it has ordered the contract of employment to continue. However, these have been in unusual circumstances as in *Hill* v. *CA Parsons* (1972).

Rescission

KEY DEFINITION

Rescission: this remedy restores the parties to their position before the contract or other transaction was made.

EXAM TIP

You are unlikely to get a detailed question on this but a knowledge of it is useful as it is the normal remedy in cases of undue influence.

Rectification

KEY DEFINITION

Where a written instrument (e.g. a contract) does not accord with the actual intentions of the parties it can be made to do so by an order of **rectification**.

KEY CASE

***Craddock Bros.* v. *Hunt* [1923] 2 Ch 136 (HC)**

Concerning: rectification

Facts

A conveyance of a house included the adjacent yard, which actually belonged to another house.

Legal principle

The conveyance would be rectified to exclude the yard.

Equitable doctrines

We will now consider the following equitable doctrines:

- undue influence
- confidence.

There are other equitable doctrines but you are less likely to be asked questions on them. Their names, so that you can check if they are on your syllabus, are:

- conversion
- reconversion
- election
- performance
- satisfaction.

Undue influence

Undue influence is a doctrine that, by its nature, is difficult to define precisely but in essence it aims to prevent the vulnerable from exploitation. It is really directed at the manner in which a transaction is entered into.

Example one

A wealthy elderly lady, Florence, has become a recluse and relies for advice on her accountant, Tom, who is the only person she sees regularly apart from her carers. She tells the accountant that she intends to make a will but has no one to leave her property to. Tom says that he will give the matter some thought and, in the course of many conversations, gradually persuades her to leave a substantial part of her property to him. A straightforward example of undue influence is *Re Craig* (1971).

KEY CASE

***Royal Bank of Scotland* v. *Etridge (No.2)* [2001] UKHL 44 (HL)**

Concerning: what is undue influence?

Facts

The facts of this case do not aid an understanding of the legal principle.

Legal principle

Lord Nicholls (HL) held that there is a distinction between:

(a) cases of actual coercion
(b) cases where the undue influence arises from a particular relationship.

In (b) there is a subdivision between:

(i) Cases where there is a relationship of trust between them and confidence between two people. If it is established that there has been a transaction which calls for some explanation then the burden shifts to the person seeking to uphold the transaction to produce evidence to counter the inference of undue influence.
(ii) Certain types of relationship where one party has acquired influence over another who is vulnerable and dependent and by whom substantial gifts are not normally to be expected (e.g. parent and child, trustee and beneficiary and medical adviser and patient). In these cases there is a presumption of undue influence by the stronger party over the weaker. *Goodchild* v. *Bradbury* (2006) appears to be an example of this category.

EXAM TIP

The most likely area of undue influence for problem questions is (b)(ii) above. It should be noted that (b)(i) does not include husband and wife, a common scenario for exam problems and so this situation would fall into (b)(ii).

Problem area: The presumption of undue influence

Having first decided that this is a possible undue influence case, you should move on immediately to see where in the above categories it falls. This will decide the rest of the case as it is vital to know if undue influence has to be proved or not.

Undue influence and third parties

This area has become of great importance in recent years especially since the decision of the House of Lords in *Barclays Bank* v. *O'Brien* (1994).

Students often jump straight to this issue when they see it in a problem question and do not first ask if there has been undue influence in the first place. Do this first!

Example two

John persuades Claud, his partner, to enter into a second mortgage of their jointly owned home to the Viper Bank in order to secure some business debts of John. It is clear that John exercised undue influence over Claud to persuade him to sign. The question is whether the Viper Bank is affected by what John has done. If it is not, then although John may be liable to Claud the actual mortgage is unaffected.

EXAM TIP

The principles stated by Lord Browne-Wilkinson in *Barclays Bank* v. *O'Brien* (1994) were the starting point of the law here. However, they have been overtaken by those stated by Lord Nicholls in Etridge (below) and in a problem question you should concentrate on applying these.

Note: In the case below the word 'surety' is used and here it means the person who has agreed to guarantee the debt, etc.: Claud in the above example.

KEY CASE

***Royal Bank of Scotland* v. *Etridge (No.2)* [2002] 2 AC 773 (HL)**

Concerning: (a) when a lender is put on inquiry and (b) steps which a lender should take to avoid being affected by the undue influence of another (e.g. the borrower)

Facts

The facts of this case do not aid an understanding of the legal principle.

KEY CASE

Legal principles

These were stated by Lord Nicholls as follows:

(a) A lender is put on inquiry when one person offers to stand surety for the debts of:

- his or her spouse
- a person involved in a non-commercial relationship with the surety and the lender is aware of this
- any company in which any of the above hold shares.

(b) Steps to be taken when a lender is put on inquiry:

- The lender must contact the surety and request that they nominate a solicitor.
- The surety must reply nominating a solicitor.
- The lender must, with the consent of the surety, disclose to the solicitor all relevant information – both the debtor's financial position and the details of the proposed loan.
- The solicitor must advise the surety in a face-to-face meeting at which the debtor is not present. The advice must cover an explanation of the documentation, the risks to the surety in signing and emphasise that the surety must decide whether to proceed.
- The solicitor must, if satisfied that the surety wishes to proceed, send written confirmation to the lender that the solicitor has explained the nature of the documents and their implications for the surety.

FURTHER THINKING

The principle in *O'Brien* and the decision in *Etridge* (above) have been the subject of a great deal of academic debate. A good place to start is the article by Andrews (2002).

Consequences of undue influence

If the transaction is affected by undue influence then it is voidable.

Problem area: The extent to which the mortgage is set aside

- *TSB* v. *Camfield* (1995): the whole mortgage was set aside.
- *Dunbar Bank plc* v. *Nadeem* (1997): it was only set aside on condition that the claimant accounted to the mortgagee for the benefit which she had from it.

Misrepresentation and undue influence

Instead of or in addition to the possibility of undue influence an exam question may ask you if there has been misrepresentation. You will probably not need to remember so much on this as you did in your contract days, but do note the definition:

KEY DEFINITION

Misrepresentation is an untrue statement of fact which induces a person to enter into a transaction.

Look out for where undue influence and **misrepresentation** are possibly combined: i.e. X uses undue influence to persuade Y, his partner, to sign a mortgage but also lies about how much, for example, the mortgage is for.

FURTHER THINKING

Read 'Mortgages and Undue Influence' (Thompson, 2003). It provides an excellent critical study of the law.

Confidence

In *Stephens* v. *Avery* (1988) Browne-Wilkinson V-C said that:

> 'the basis of equitable intervention to protect confidentiality is that it is unconscionable for a person who has received (confidential) information . . . subsequently to reveal that information'.

Thus the duty of confidentiality does not depend on the existence of any contract or other legal relationship.

KEY CASE

***A-G* v. *Guardian Newspapers Ltd (No. 2)* [1988] 3 All ER 545 (HL)**

Concerning: operation of the duty of confidence

Facts

The Crown sought to limit publication of memoirs (called '*Spycatcher*') by a former member of the secret service.

Legal principle

Lord Goff stated that there were three limiting principles to the operation of the doctrine:

KEY CASE

1 When the information has entered the 'public domain' it cannot, as general rule, be regarded as confidential.
2 The duty does not apply to useless or trivial information.
3 The duty of confidence may be outweighed by a greater public interest in its disclosure (but see *Venables* below).

KEY CASE

***Venables* v. *News Group Newspapers Ltd* [2001] 1 All ER 908 (HC)**

Concerning: actions for breach of confidence and the Human Rights Act

Facts

Two ten-year-old boys (the claimants) had been convicted of the murder of James Bulger, a little boy of two, in shocking circumstances. When they were about to be released on parole there was concern that their own lives could be in danger in view of the very strong feelings which their killing of James had aroused. Therefore injunctions world-wide were sought which would prohibit the publication of information leading to the identification of the claimants' whereabouts.

Legal principle

The court granted the injunction on the basis that there was a real risk of harm to the claimants and was greatly influenced by the effect of the European Convention on Human Rights (ECHR). Although Article 10 of the ECHR guarantees freedom of expression, the counter argument for an injunction to maintain confidentiality was bolstered by Article 2 (the right to life, as without an injunction the lives of the claimants would be in danger), by Article 3 (the right not to be subjected to torture or inhuman or degrading treatment as this could also occur) and by Article 8 (the right to respect for private and family life).

Chapter summary
Putting it all together

TEST YOURSELF

- [ ] Can you tick all the points from the **revision checklist** at the beginning of this chapter?
- [ ] Take the **end-of-chapter quiz** on the companion website.
- [ ] Test your knowledge of the cases with the **revision flashcards** on the website.
- [ ] Attempt the **essay question** from the beginning of this chapter using the guidelines below.
- [ ] Go to the companion website to try out **other questions**.

Answer guidelines

See the essay question at the start of this chapter.

It is a very typical one in equity exams and requires you to think about the nature of equitable remedies. What you must *not* do is to just plough through the remedies summarising them!

Instead you must start with an Introduction which addresses the issue: what is meant by discretionary? Look back to *Patel* v. *Ali* and discuss how the word 'discretionary' was applied. The essential point is that, although there are no rigid rules about when equitable remedies will be granted and refused, there are principles.

Now go on to select cases illustrating principles in the grant of equitable remedies – look back through the material in this chapter and select cases which you think that you can use and then research them.

Make your answer stand out

Go to Chapter 9 on constructive trusts and refer to the remedial constructive trust. This is said to be a remedy. Is it? If it is, it is certainly discretionary but what are the principles which govern its exercise? Are there any?.

FURTHER READING

Andrews, G. (2002) 'Undue Influence – Where's the disadvantage?', 66 Conv. 456.

Dockray, M. and Laddie, H. (1990) 'Piller Problems', 106 LQR 661.

Phang, A. (1998) 'Specific Performance – Explaining the Roots of Settled Practice', 61 MLR 421.

Thompson, M. (2003) 'Mortgages and Undue Influence', in *Modern Studies in Property Law*, (ed. Cooke), 2nd edn, Oxford: Hart Publishing.

3 The three certainties

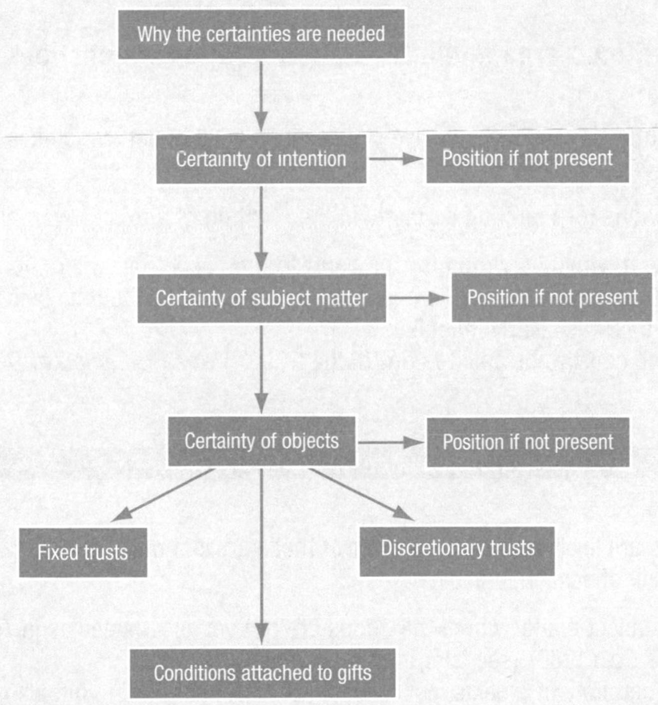

A printable version of this topic map is available from www.pearsoned.co.uk/lawexpress

Revision Checklist

Essential points you should know:

- [ ] why the certainties are needed
- [ ] what the three certainties are
- [ ] the distinction between fixed and discretionary trusts
- [ ] the distinction between where property is left on trust and where there is a conditional gift
- [ ] the effect of a clause which attempts to cure uncertainty.

Introduction:
Understanding the three certainties

This is not a difficult area and often appears in exam questions.

Three certainties questions usually involve clauses in wills although certainties issues can arise in *inter vivos* gifts also.

There are two reasons for requiring certainty in the creation of a trust:

1 A practical one. It would be wrong for the court to impose a trust where none was intended. Trusteeship can be an onerous task and so no one should be held a trustee unless this was clearly intended.
2 The need for the court to be able to control the trust (*Morice* v. *Bishop of Durham* (1805)).

Assessment advice

Essay questions

Essay questions are likely to deal with either of these areas, both of which have led to a great deal of academic debate:

- certainty of subject matter where the goods are not yet ascertained as in *Re London Wine Co.* (1986) (see later in this chapter)
- the tests for certainty of objects, especially in discretionary trusts but also possibly in fixed trusts and where there is a condition precedent. The decisions in *McPhail* v. *Doulton* [1971] and *Re Barlow's Will Trusts* (1979) are worth looking at in detail. Make sure that you understand the debates surrounding them.

Assessment advice

Problem questions

The three certainties is one of the favourite areas for problem questions. These are not difficult to gain a reasonable pass on but if you are looking for a really good mark you need to go deeper than just running through the requirements of certainty and concentrate on discussing any problematic areas such as those mentioned in the essay question advice above. You can also boost your mark in answering problem questions by paying very close attention to the actual words used in the creation of a trust and analysing them very carefully. To sum up: this is a good area to aim to score highly on.

Sample question

Could you answer this question? Below is a typical problem question that could arise on this topic. An outline answer is included at the end of the chapter, whilst a sample essay question and guidance on tackling it can be found on the companion website.

Problem question

Susan, who died recently, left a will containing the following bequests:

(a) £250,000 to my husband, John, safe in the knowledge that he will provide for our children.

(b) £10,000 to my daughter, Barbara, provided that she allows my sister, Eileen, a reasonable sum each year to provide her with a few of the little comforts of life.

(c) My collection of rare books shall be available for any friend of mine who wishes to select a book in memory of me.

(d) £300,000 to be distributed, at the discretion of my trustees, amongst employees, ex-employees, their friends and relations of my late husband's company, Midland Optical Illusion Ltd.

Can you advise Arthur, Susan's executor, on the validity of these gifts?

What are the three certainties?

These are:

- certainty of intention to create a trust
- certainty of the subject matter of the trust
- certainty of the objects of the trust.

These requirements have been set out in many cases, for example, by Lord Langdale in *Knight* v. *Knight* (1840).

Certainty of intention

Certainty of intention means that the person who is given the property shall hold it on trust, i.e. it is evidence that the settlor or testator intended to impose a binding obligation that the property was to be held on trust. Often common sense and an ability to see clearly what precise words and phrases mean is enough when answering a problem question.

Example one

(a) John by will leaves £1,000 to Albert and says that he would like Albert to look after his children.
(b) John leaves £1,000 to Albert on trust for his children.

It is obvious that (b) is a trust but that (a) is not. Why? Because in (a) there is only a request. It is often said that 'precatory words do not create a trust'. Precatory words are words such as request, hope and desire which do not impose a trust and where the recipient can keep the property as a gift. A good example is *Re Diggles* (1888) where the word desire did not create a trust.

EXAM TIP

- Use your common sense – do the words used look like the imposition of a trust?
- Look at all the words used – not just particular ones.

Compare the following cases:

KEY CASE

***Re Adams and Kensington Vestry* (1884) 27 Ch D 394 (CA)**

Concerning: certainty of intention

Facts

The testator gave his estate to his wife 'in full confidence that she will do what is right as the disposal thereof between my children . . .'.

Legal principle

The words 'in full confidence' did not create a trust.

KEY CASE

***Comiskey* v. *Bowring-Hanbury* [1905] AC 84 (HL)**

Concerning: certainty of intention

Facts

A testator gave his property to his wife 'in full confidence that at her death she will devise it to one or more of my nieces as she shall think fit'. If she did not do this then the will directed that the property should be divided equally among the nieces. It was held that this created a trust.

Legal principle

Look at the meaning of the words used taken as a whole and not in isolation. Although the words 'in full confidence' were used here as in *Adams* (above), here the second sentence was clearly mandatory and so created a trust.

KEY CASE

***Re Harding* (2007) EWHC 3 (HC)**

Concerning: certainty of intention to create a trust

Facts

The testatrix's will said that it was her wish that all she possessed should be taken by the Roman Catholic Diocese of Westminster to hold in trust for the Black Community in four London Boroughs. Did these words create a trust?

Legal principle

The court held that they did. Although the word 'wish' was in itself precatory the will did use the word 'trust' later.

FURTHER THINKING

Learn some more modern examples of equity in this area (e.g. *R* v. *Clowes* (No.2) [1994]). This also illustrates a link between equity and the law of theft: you can impress the examiner with your knowledge of this! In *Duggan* v. *Governor of Full Sutton Prison* (2004) it was held that when prisoners' money was put in a fund under the control of the governor there was no intention to create a trust of that money for the prisoners. *Paul* v. *Constance* [1977] (see Chapter 6) is a good example for exams as you can combine it with a discussion of constitution of trusts. See *Re Farepak Food and Gifts Ltd* (*in administation*) (2006) in Chapter 8. This is an excellent case for essay questions as it contains material on express, resulting and constructive trusts.

The *effect* of the lack of certainty of intention is that the donee (no trustee here) takes the property as an absolute gift.

Certainty of subject matter

This is a simple enough point: there is no point in creating a trust by showing certainty of intention if we do not know what property is to be held on trust.

KEY CASE

***Anthony* v. *Donges* (1998) 2 FLR 775 (HC)**

Concerning: certainty of subject matter

Facts

A widow was left 'such minimal part of the estate as she might be entitled to . . . for maintenance purposes'.

Legal principle

There was no certainty of subject matter.

See also *Palmer* v. *Simmonds* (1854): 'the bulk of my estate' was too uncertain.

KEY CASE

***Re Golay* [1965] 1 WLR 969**

Concerning: apparent lack of certainty of subject matter

Facts

Executors under a will were directed to allow a beneficiary 'to enjoy the use of one of my flats and receive a reasonable income from my other properties'.

Legal principle

Although the word 'reasonable' seemed too uncertain the gift was upheld as the court assumed that it referred to the beneficiaries' previous standard of living.

KEY CASE

***Curtis* v. *Rippon* (1820) 5 Madd 434 (HC)**

Concerning: the possibility that a person is intended to be a trustee of part but to receive the other part as a gift

Facts

A widow received all her husband's property subject to a trust where she was to 'use the property for her spiritual and temporal good and that of the children, remembering always according to circumstances the Church of God and the poor'. It was held that as the shares to be taken by the children, the Church and the poor were uncertain, the widow took all as there was no doubt that she was intended to benefit to some extent.

Legal principle

Where the shares to be taken by the beneficiaries are uncertain but there is also an absolute gift (often to the intended trustee) then the gift takes effect.

Students sometimes say at this point: 'But it is a fundamental principle that a trustee cannot benefit from the trust.' Quite right. But the point is that there is no trust as there is no certainty of subject matter.

KEY CASE

***Re London Wine Co. Shippers Ltd* [1986] PCC 121 (HC)**

Concerning: certainty of subject matter where goods are unascertained

Facts

Buyers of wine which was stored at a warehouse claimed that it was held on trust for them but the claim failed as the wine had not been separated from a larger stock of similar wine held at the warehouse.

Legal principle

Trust property must be ascertainable.

FURTHER THINKING

Look also, for example, at *Hunter* v. *Moss* (1994) and *Re Goldcorp Exchange Ltd (in receivership)* [1995]. Read the criticism of *Hunter* v. *Moss* by Hayton (1994).

The *effect* of the lack of certainty of subject matter is:

- if there is no certainty of what the subject matter is then there can be no trust as there is nothing to hold on trust
- if the attempted trust has been attached to a gift then the gift becomes absolute as in *Curtis* v. *Rippon* (1820) (above).

Certainty of objects (i.e. beneficiaries)

Note at the outset that the rules differ depending on the type of trust (see Figure 3.1):

Figure 3.1

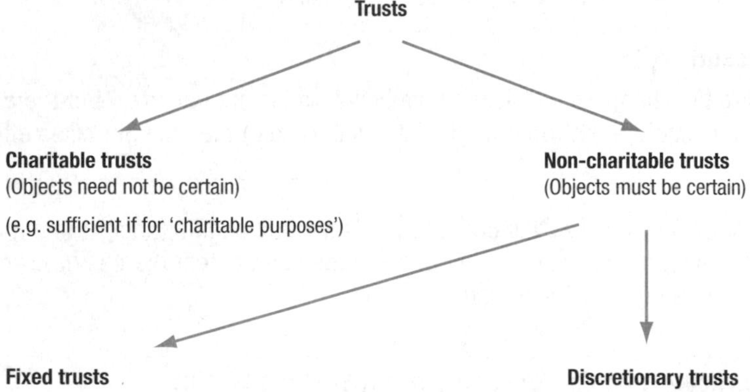

This chapter will deal with non-charitable trusts (private trusts) as one exam question would be unlikely to deal with certainties in both charitable and non-charitable trusts.

REVISION NOTE

Check Chapter 8 for certainty of objects in charitable trusts.

It is vital that you recognise and can apply the distinction between fixed and discretionary trusts.

Fixed trusts

KEY DEFINITION

A **fixed trust** is one where the interests in the trust property are fixed in the trust instrument.

Example two

'To all my children in equal shares.'
Here there is no room for any discretion by the trustees.

KEY DEFINITION

Rule for certainty of objects in fixed trusts: All the beneficiaries must be capable of being listed, i.e. there must be no doubt as to who the beneficiaries are: *IRC* v. *Broadway Cottages Trust* (1955).

This is really common sense when applied to the above example. Each child is to have an equal amount and so the division cannot be made until we know how many to divide the sum by.

KEY DEFINITION

A **discretionary trust** is one where the trustees have a discretion as to whether a person will be a beneficiary or not.

KEY CASE

***McPhail* v. *Doulton* [1971] AC 424 (HL)**

Concerning: certainty of objects in discretionary trusts

Facts

A trust provided that the trustees were to apply the income from a fund at their absolute discretion for the benefit of any officers and employees of a (named) company together with ex-officers and ex-employees and their relatives and dependants. This was sufficiently certain.

Legal principle

In discretionary trusts the test for certainty of objects is: 'Can it be said with certainty that any given individual is or is not a member of the class?' (Lord Wilberforce)

KEY DEFINITION

Rule for certainty of objects in discretionary trusts: 'Can it be said with certainty that any given individual is or is not a member of the class?'

As you can see from the facts it would be impossible to list all the beneficiaries (e.g. who are the relatives?). However, it must be possible to say with certainty if a particular person is a beneficiary.

Example three

A gift to my old mates. This does not satisfy the test of certainty as it is not possible to say with certainty if anyone is an old mate.

Example four

A gift to my cousins. This does satisfy the test, as it is possible to say with certainty if a person is a cousin.

Conceptual and evidential uncertainty

Re Baden's Deed Trusts (No.2) [1973] distinguished between conceptual and evidential uncertainty. Example three is a case of conceptual uncertainty in that the whole concept of a mate is not capable of precise definition and so the gift will fail. Example four is an example of evidential uncertainty in that it may be difficult to establish who is a cousin but that is no bar to a person coming forward and proving that she *is* a cousin.

Effect of a lack of certainty

Provided that the other two certainties are present the property will be held on a resulting trust for the settlor or, if the trust is created by will, then for the testator's estate.

Note these other points in certainty of objects in discretionary trusts:

- *Trustees have a duty to appreciate the 'width of the field'* (Megarry VC in *Re Hay's Settlement Trusts* [1982]). This means that although they cannot draw up a complete list of the objects they should not distribute the property until they have decided if the selection is to be made 'merely from a dozen or instead, thousands or millions'.
- There is some authority for saying that the trust will not be enforced if the width of objects makes it 'administratively unworkable'. In *R* v. *District Auditor, ex parte West Yorkshire MCC* [1986] a trust for the inhabitants of West Yorkshire (about 2.5 million people) failed on this ground.

Power to cure uncertainty

This can arise in two situations:

(a) Where there is uncertainty about a particular *fact*. A third party can be made judge of this.

KEY CASE

Re Tuck's Settlement Trusts **[1978] Ch 49 (HC)**

Concerning: decision on whether a person satisfies a criteria to be made by a third party

Facts

A Chief Rabbi was made judge of whether a person was of Jewish blood.

Legal principle

This was valid as the decision was to be based on measurable criteria.

(b) Where there is conceptual uncertainty.

Example five

John's will provides that each of his old drinking pals at the Black Bush shall have a bottle of whisky and that, in case of doubt, the landlord of the Black Bush shall have the power to decide who they are.

Given that the phrase 'old drinking pals at the Black Bush' is conceptually uncertain, does the power given to the landlord save it?

The probability is that this would not save the gift as the point is that the phrase itself is conceptually uncertain and so a power to decide is irrelevant: What can the landlord decide? In addition, the court cannot control the trust (e.g. see *Re Jones* [1953]).

Conditions precedent and certainty of objects

KEY CASE

***Re Barlow's Will Trusts* (1979) 1 WLR 278 (HC)**

Concerning: certainty of objects where there is a condition precedent

Facts

A will directed that a friend of the testator should be allowed to purchase any of her paintings. The court held that a friend was a person who had met the testator frequently when circumstances allowed on a social and not a business occasion. On this basis the gift was allowed to stand.

Legal principle

Gifts subject to conditions precedent are subject to a less strict test than those in discretionary trusts as the amount which one person receives does not affect what others will receive.

FURTHER THINKING

This case is controversial and you should be prepared to discuss if it is correct. See Emery (1982) for an excellent article that goes to the heart of the issues.

EXAM TIP

Students often apply the test in *Re Barlow's Will Trusts* [1979] whenever they see the word 'friend' in a question. This may be wrong. If £100 is left to be shared on discretionary trusts 'among all my friends' this would fail as the test in *McPhail* v. *Doulton* (1971) would apply and friends would not satisfy it.

The rule against perpetuities and discretionary trusts

REVISION NOTE

This rule is dealt with in Chapter 4 but for now just remember that it may come up in a certainties question!

Chapter summary: **Putting it all together**

TEST YOURSEL F

- [ ] Can you tick all the points from the **revision checklist** at the beginning of this chapter?
- [ ] Take the **end-of-chapter quiz** on the companion website.
- [ ] Test your knowledge of the cases with the **revision flashcards** on the website.
- [ ] Attempt the **essay question** from the beginning of this chapter using the guidelines below.
- [ ] Go to the companion website to try out **other questions**.

Answer guidelines

See the problem question at the start of the chapter.

A diagram illustrating how to structure your answer is available on the website.

Note carefully exactly what the question asks you to do. Here it asks you to advise on the validity of the gifts. If the gifts are not valid trusts then who gets them? Always find a home for the property! Make it a habit to check at the end of answering a certainties question (and other trusts questions) that you have decided where the property will go to.

Deal with all three certainties when looking at each situation, even if in some cases the answer is so obvious that you do not spend much time on some areas.

Never waste time in dealing with the question of the validity of the will. Do not set out the formalities for a valid will unless the question asks you to do this. Assume that the will is valid and go straight to the certainties issues unless directed otherwise. It would be very unlikely that some issue of the validity of the will would arise in a question like this.

Regarding part (a). 'Safe in the knowledge': this may not satisfy the requirement of certainty of intention. Look at the cases (e.g. *Re Adams and Kensington Vestry*) and decide if it indicates the imposition of a trust. If there is no trust there will be an absolute gift to John.

Regarding part (b). There is probably certainty of intention: 'provided that', although this should be discussed. The problem is that there appears to be no certainty of subject matter unless the principle in *Re Golay* applies and external evidence can establish what a reasonable sum is – the words 'a few of the little comforts of life' may help here. If no trust then the whole sum will go to Barbara.

Regarding part (c). Can the *Re Barlow* principle apply? This seems to be a conditional gift as being a friend is a condition of selecting a book. If so, then provided that the court is prepared to lay down conditions for friendship the gift will be valid.

Regarding part (d). There is no doubt of certainty of intention and subject matter (but gain a few marks by just pointing this out) but is there certainty of objects? A close look at *McPhail* v. *Doulton* is needed here, as this is a discretionary trust. Mention and apply the distinction between evidential and conceptual uncertainty. Probably valid. If not, a resulting trust for Susan's estate.

Make your answer stand out

Analyse the situation in (b) very carefully and explain the decision in *Re Barlow* and any problems associated with it very clearly.

FURTHER READING

Emery, C. (1982) 'The Most Hallowed Principle', 98 LQR 551.
Harris, J. (1971) 'Trust, Power and Duty', 87 LQR 31. This analyses the decision in *McPhail* v. *Doulton*.
Hayton, D. (1994) 'Uncertainty of Subject Matter of Trusts', 110 LQR 335.

4 The beneficiary principle and purpose trusts

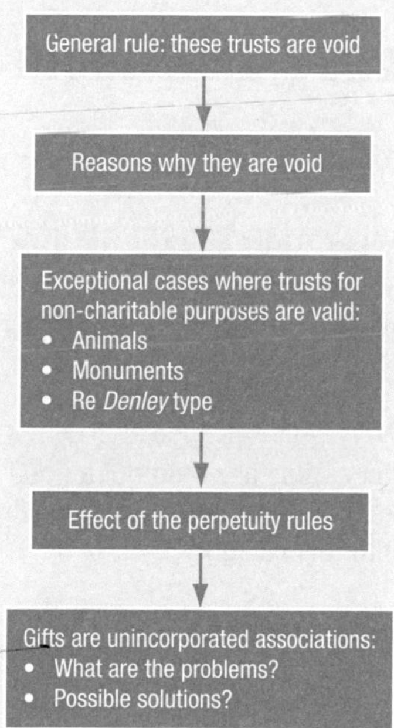

A printable version of this topic map is available from www.pearsoned.co.uk/lawexpress

Revision Checklist

Essential points you should know:

- [ ] why non-charitable purpose trusts are generally held void
- [ ] the special rules on trusts for animals and monuments and the principle in *Re Denley*
- [ ] what the rules against perpetuities are (in brief) and how they affect these trusts
- [ ] what an unincorporated association is and why gifts to them cause problems
- [ ] the possible solutions: trust for members or gift to the members on a contractual basis
- [ ] the ways of disposing of surplus funds of unincorporated associations.

Introduction:
Understanding non-charitable purpose trusts

The fact that this is a complex area should not put you off answering a question on it because examiners, knowing that the topic is complex, will reward candidates who make a decent attempt at the question.

You should not attempt a question on this area without a good knowledge of charitable trusts, as your answer will require you to explain why the trust is not charitable, which is why it falls into this category.

Assessment advice

Essay questions

An essay question will almost certainly focus on the reasons why non-charitable purpose trusts are generally held to be void and so you will need not only a good knowledge of the law but also of thinking in this area.

Assessment advice

Problem questions

A problem question may involve one or more gifts and ask you to decide if they are valid. You will need to explain why they are not valid charitable gifts, although this should not occupy too much of your time as the question is not a charity one. You may decide to investigate if the gift could take effect as a valid private trust and here you will need to investigate if it satisfies the rules on certainty of objects (see Chapter 3). This is well worth doing as it shows the examiner that you are thinking laterally, although only do so if there is a reasonable possibility of a valid private trust. The other possibility is that it may be a gift to an unincorporated association in which case the law is the same as for other non-charitable purpose trusts but will need to be approached from a different angle. In both situations you will also need to mention the application of the rule against perpetuities.

Sample question

Could you answer this question? Below is a typical problem question that could arise on this topic. Guidelines on answering the question are included at the end of this chapter, whilst a sample essay question and guidance on tackling it can be found on the companion website.

Problem question

John wishes to make a will under which:

(a) £10,000 is left for the maintenance of his tomb in the churchyard of St Catherine's Church Droitwich
(b) £1000 is left for the maintenance of his dog, Hugo
(c) £20,000 is left to the Hanbury Cricket Club to build a new pavilion
(d) £50,000 is left to the Worcester Branch of the XYZ Political Party.

Can you advise John on whether and to what extent his wishes can be carried out.

General rule for non-charitable purpose trusts

The general rule is that these trusts are void.

KEY CASE

***Re Astor's Settlement Trusts* [1952] Ch 534 (HC)**

Concerning: non-charitable purpose trusts

Facts

A trust was established for various purposes including the maintenance of good relations between nations and the preservation of the independence of newspapers.

Legal principle

The trust was void. It was for non-charitable purposes (it was not even argued that they were charitable) and there was no one who could enforce the trust.

REVISION NOTE

Go to Chapter 10 and see why these purposes were not charitable.

This was the first time that the courts clearly held that these trusts were void. Why was this so? The best way is to set these trusts in the context of trusts in general (see Figure 4.1).

Figure 4.1

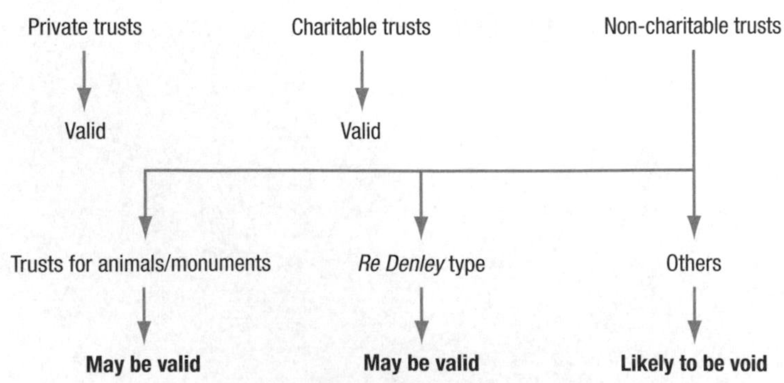

You need to remember that Figure 4.1 is only a sketch and that various details need to be fitted in but it should guide you through this area.

Reasons why these trusts are void

Look at Figure 4.1 and consider the following two points:

1 *A trust must have someone who can compel performance of it* (the beneficiary principle).
2 The origin of this principle is in a statement of Grant MR in *Morice* v. *Bishop of Durham* (1805).

How do the trusts in Figure 4.1 fare?

- A private trust can be enforced by the beneficiaries.
- A charitable trust can be enforced by the Attorney-General.
- A non-charitable purpose trust has no one to enforce it.

The objects of a trust (except a charitable trust) must be expressed with sufficient certainty to enable the court to control it. This is really another way of looking at the issue raised by the beneficiary principle: the need for the court to be able to control the trust.

If the objects of the trust in *Re Astor* were not carried out, who would be able to take action? Even if there was someone to argue in court that there was a breach of these trusts, could the court tell if this was so? If all the trust funds in *Re Astor* were being spent on the promotion of war instead of peace then the court could no doubt find a breach but look at some of the other cases below and see if the court could decide if there was a breach.

The principle in *Re Astor* has been applied to:

- a trust for the purposes of a contemplative order of nuns (*Leahy* v. *A-G for New South Wales* [1959])

REVISION NOTE

Go to Chapter 10 and look at *Gilmour* v. *Coates* and note the similarity between it and *Leahy*.

- a trust for the Labour Party (*Re Grant's Will Trusts* [1979])
- a trust to provide a useful memorial (*Re Endacott* [1960]).

In the rest of this chapter we shall refer to the *Re Astor* principle as the 'beneficiary principle'.

FURTHER THINKING

See Chapter 1 of *Trends in Contemporary Trust Law* (Matthews, 1996). If you are aiming for an above average mark on this question then you must read further than the textbooks on the issues involved here and this chapter is the place to start.

The way forward is now to look at:

- ways in which the courts have tried to limit the scope of the beneficiary principle
- ways in which the beneficiary principle comes into conflict with other rules and concepts
- ways in which the law might develop in the future.

Return to Figure 4.1. You will see that it mentions two situations where these trusts may be valid and you need to consider them in more detail.

Exceptions to the beneficiary principle

Trusts to care for animals and for the upkeep of specific monuments

This is an anomaly. Remember that *Re Astor* was the first case where the beneficiary principle was held to invalidate trusts for non-charitable purposes. Thus before then, although it was realised that there were objections to them, there was some freedom for the courts to develop the law as they saw fit. This explains this exception.

Some cases are *Re Hooper* [1932] (monuments) and *Re Dean* (1889) (animals).

Note that the courts now confine these cases within narrow limits: for example, a gift to maintain an animal and also to breed from it would not be valid – breeding would take it beyond caring. This is a common examination point.

Note also *Re Endacott* [1960]: an example of the unwillingness of the courts to extend the law here (see page 49).

Trusts of the *Re Denley* type

KEY CASE

***Re Denley's Trust Deed* [1969] 1 Ch 373 (HC)**

Concerning: validity of a trust which appeared to be primarily for purposes and not persons

Facts

Land was conveyed to trustees to hold it for the purpose of a recreation or sports ground primarily for the benefit of the employees of a company and then for the benefit of such other person(s) as the trustees might allow.

Legal principle

The trust was valid as it was for the benefit of the employees and it was not a purpose trust.

EXAM TIP

Examiners will expect you to be able to analyse the issues in this case so be prepared and read, for example, Everton (1982).

Ways in which the beneficiary principle comes into conflict with other rules and concepts

Figure 4.2

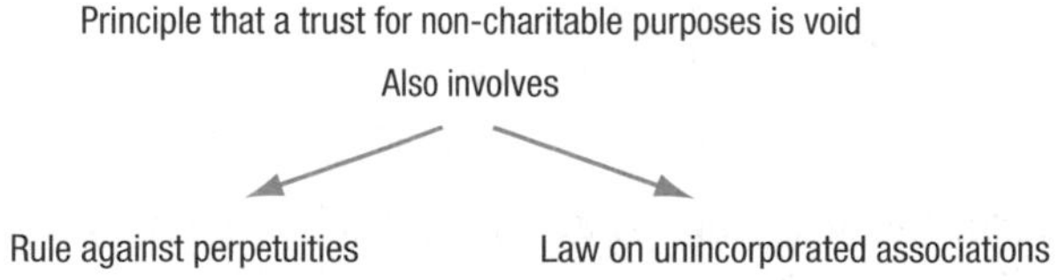

Principle that a trust for non-charitable purposes is void

Also involves

Rule against perpetuities

Law on unincorporated associations

Having learnt the rule and the exceptions to the beneficiary principle you now need to be able to appreciate how it comes into collision with two other areas: the perpetuity rules and gifts to unincorporated associations (see Figure 4.2).

Effect of the perpetuity rules

Example one

John leaves £1000 to Tim on trust to care for the monument over his tombstone. When is the trust to end? When Tim dies it is possible for new trustees to be appointed but this is not the point. When will the trust end?

The law feels that non-charitable purpose trusts should have a lifespan. The rule against perpetuities fixes this.

KEY DEFINITION

The **Rule against Perpetuities** (in this context) provides that a gift to be held for a non-charitable purpose trust is void if it may last beyond lives or lives in being plus 21 years (see s.15(4) of the Perpetuities and Accumulations Act 1964).

In fact, the courts have tried to ensure that these trusts do not fall foul of the principle. See *Mussett* v. *Bingle* (1876) regarding the assumption that a monument would be erected within the perpetuity period.

Where a trust states that it is to last for 'as long as the law allows' this will be taken to be the perpetuity period and so it will be valid.

Note: *Re Haines* (1952) – the courts take judicial notice of the lifespan of particular animals. Here that a cat could not live beyond 21 years. Thus the gift was valid.

Gifts to unincorporated associations

Problem area: Validity of gifts to unincorporated associations

This can be a difficult area in problem questions as it involves the following three areas:

1 beneficiary principle
2 rule against perpetuities
3 nature of unincorporated associations.

Keep each point distinct and apply separately to the question.

The fundamental point is that unincorporated associations do not exist in law and so any gift must be for their purposes.
Although Barbara may think she has made a gift to the club itself, she has not.

REVISION NOTE

Go to Chapter 8 and check that you are clear on the law on the disposal of the surplus funds of unincorporated associations.

Example two

Figure 4.3

Although Barbara may think she has made a gift to the club itself, she has not Assuming that it is not a registered company, the club is an unincorporated association and so does not exist.

The next question is whether the club can be a charity.

REVISION NOTE

Go to Chapter 10 and check on the purposes which can be charitable.

Under the Charities Act 2006 if the club is amateur the gift can be for charitable purposes and be valid.

Let us assume that the Hanbury FC is semi-professional. Here we have a problem as the gift is for non-charitable purposes and must be held on trust, but these trusts are void. The same would apply if the gift had been made to a political party.

FURTHER THINKING

The fact that there are legal difficulties with these gifts has caused adverse comment. A good example is:

> 'It would astonish a layman to be told that there was a difficulty in his giving a legacy to an unincorporated non-charitable society which he had or could have supported without difficulty in his lifetime'.
>
> (Brightman J in *Re Recher's Will Trusts* [1972])

The result is that the courts have tried to find ways of making these gifts valid. There are two possibilities:

1 a gift on trust for the benefit of the members – see *Re Denley* above
2 a gift to the members who will hold it on the basis of the contract between them contained in the rules of the association.

These possibilities often form part of a problem question in an exam. We need now to look at them carefully.

KEY CASE

***Re Recher's Will Trusts* [1972] Ch 526 (HC)**

Concerning: validity of gifts to unincorporated associations

Facts

A gift was made to the London and Provincial Anti-Vivisection Society, a non-charitable association.

Legal principle

This was valid as it was a gift to the members as an addition to the funds subject to the contract between them as set out in the rules. It was not an immediate gift to the members.

Compare this with *Re Lipinski's Will Trusts* (1976).

KEY CASE

***Re Horley Town Football Club; Hunt* v. *McLaren* (2006) EWHC 2386 (HC)**

Concerning: validity of gifts to unincorporated associations

Facts

The club was an unincorporated association. In 1948 the then president of the club had settled land on trust to secure a permanent endowment for the club and in 2002 the land was sold and the proceeds used to buy other land and provide sports facilities. A surplus remained and the issue was the precise basis on which the assets of the club were held.

Legal principle

The trust deed of 1948 should be interpreted as a gift to the club as a contract-holding gift to the club members for the time being. The beneficial interest vested in the current full members and was held on a bare trust for them. This entitled them to call in a general meeting for the assets to be transferred to them as individuals. The decision follows *Re Recher* in basing the solution on contract but the device of a trust is used to solve the problem of exactly where the legal ownership of the property lies pending any distribution between the members.

FURTHER THINKING

There have not been many recent cases on this area and so a good knowledge of the above case will obviously bring extra marks in an exam. Research it! A good place to start is Luxton (2007).

But there is still a problem: the Rule against Perpetuities:

KEY CASE

Re Grant's Will Trusts **[1979] 3 All ER 359 (HC)**

Concerning: application of the Rule against Perpetuities to gifts to unincorporated non-charitable bodies

Facts

A gift was made for the purposes of the Chertsey Labour Party but the members did not control the property nor could they gain control as the rules were subject to the jurisdiction of the National Executive of the Labour Party.

Legal principle

A gift to a non-charitable unincorporated association will fail if the members are unable to divide the gift between them, as it will have to be held for the association's purposes in perpetuity.

In *Re Horley Town Football Club* (above) the actual trust deed did define a perpetuity period but perpetuity was not a problem as the interests of the members vested immediately.

Note: Another area where the apparent lack of a beneficiary could cause problems with the enforcement of a trust (although so far it seems not to have done so) is the Quistclose type of trust dealt with in Chapter 8. This is discussed in the article by Pawlowski and Summers (2007: 445).

Future development of the law

FURTHER THINKING

As essay questions are likely in this area it is absolutely vital that you read widely and think about the issues. Look at the idea of these trusts having an enforcer who will be able to take action to enforce the trust. This would solve the fundamental problem posed at the start of this chapter. See Warburton (1985) and Pawlowski and Summers (2007). The latter argue for a general recognition by English Law of the validity of non-charitable purpose trusts provided that certain conditions are satisfied, in particular, that an enforcer is named in the trust instrument who is independent of the settlor and the beneficiaires.

Chapter summary: **Putting it all together**

TEST YOURSELF

- ☐ Can you tick all the points from the **revision checklist** at the beginning of this chapter?
- ☐ Take the **end-of-chapter quiz** on the companion website.
- ☐ Test your knowledge of the cases with the **revision flashcards** on the website.
- ☐ Attempt the **essay question** from the beginning of this chapter using the guidelines below.
- ☐ Go to the companion website to try out **other questions**.

Answer guidelines

See the problem question at the start of the chapter.

A diagram illustrating how to structure your answer is available on the website.

This question requires a clear knowledge of gifts which may be invalid as non-charitable purpose trusts together with the ability to recognise and apply the perpetuity rules.

(a) Maintenance of tomb: valid in principle but note the perpetuity point. *Mussett* v. *Bingle*: this only held that the courts would assume that the tomb would be erected within the period. A gift for the maintenance of a tomb in the same case was void as it was not within the perpetuity period. Therefore probably void.

(b) Possibly valid as it is for the upkeep of a specific animal and not to breed from it. Is it void as a perpetuity though? Can the principle in *Re Haines* apply to dogs also?

(c) Can it be a trust for the benefit of the club members (*Re Denley*)? Or a gift to the members to be held on the basis of the contract between them (*Re Recher*)? Note the similarity with *Re Lipinski*.

(d) Similar issues to those in (c) but as the money is not allocated to a specific purpose there is the possibility that it may infringe the rule against perpetuities. Can the members divide the gift among themselves or are they subject to control by the political party? See *Re Grant*.

Make your answer stand out

Apply the rules in this chapter but also:

- explain the perpetuities rule clearly

- sketch in the underlying points: the beneficiary principle and the fact that in (c) and (d) these are unincorporated associations.

FURTHER READING

Brown, J. (2007) 'What are we to do with Testamentary Trusts of Imperfect Obligation?' 71 Conv. 148.

Everton, A. (1982) Conv. 118.

Luxton, P. (2007) *Re Horley Town Football Club* 71 Conv. 274.

Matthews, P. (1996) 'The New Trust: Obligations without Rights?' in *Trends in Contemporary Trust Law* ed. A. Oakley, Oxford: Oxford University Press.

Pawlowski, M. and Summers, P. (2007) 'Private Purpose Trusts – a Reform Proposal', 71 Conv. 445.

Warburton, J. (1985) 'Holding of Property by Unincorporated Associations', Conv. 318.

5 Formalities

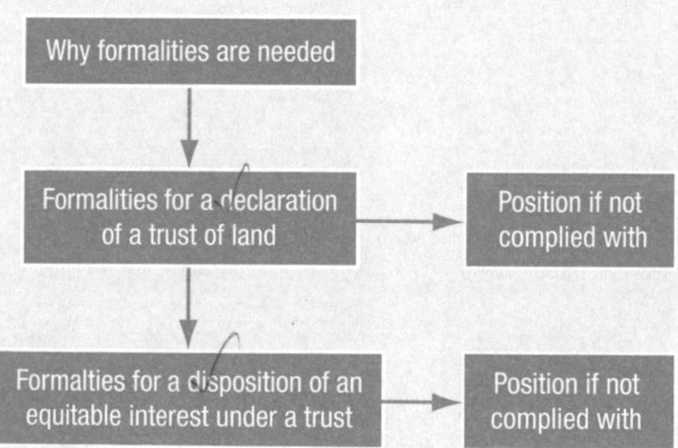

A printable version of this topic map is available from www.pearsoned.co.uk/lawexpress

Revision Checklist

Essential points you should know:

- [ ] the formalities when a trust of land is declared
- [ ] the formalities when an equitable interest under any trust is transferred
- [ ] the failure to observe these formalities: what the consequences are.

Introduction:
Understanding formalities

The basic principles are reasonably straightforward and the number of variations on them is not great.

A good attempt at a problem on formalities will be well rewarded. In addition the subject provides excellent material for essay questions.

Remember also that in order to be valid, a trust must not only comply with any requisite formalities, it must also comply with the three certainties. Check Chapter 3 and make sure that you can recall the three certainties

Assessment advice

Essay questions

Essays in this area will require you to have read and mastered the detail of the complex cases such as *Oughtred* v. *IRC* (1960) and *Vandervell* v. *IRC* (1960), and looked at the justification for these rules. You may also have a question on other areas such as constitution of a trust where you will need to deal with this area.

Problem questions

These will usually deal with a variety of situations and ask you whether the statutory provisions on the formalities will apply and, if so, what the effect of non-observance will be. Draw a diagram of the situations and remember that these types of problem questions are asking you for a sound, logical approach. Spend time before writing to get your ideas in order.

Sample question

Could you answer this question? Below is a typical problem question that could arise on this topic. Guidelines on answering the question are included at the end of this chapter, whilst a sample essay question and guidance on tackling it can be found on the companion website.

Problem question

Isabel owns a house 'The Gables' and also has £20,000 in an account at the Worcester Bank. In addition she is the beneficiary under a trust fund consisting of 1000 shares in ABC Co. Ltd, set up for her by her late father Albert, of which her brother Frank is now the trustee. She says to her son, Larry: 'In future I will hold "The Gables" for you but it will still stay in my name. The same applies to the money in the Worcester Bank.' She then rings Frank and says, 'I really do not need those shares in the ABC Co. anymore. In future pay any dividends to Larry.'

The next day Isabel dies and Hubert, her executor, asks your advice on whether and to what extent 'The Gables', the £20,000 in the bank account and the shares in the ABC Co. Ltd form part of Isabel's estate.

Declaration of a trust of land

KEY STATUTE

Law of Property Act 1925, s.53(1)(b)

'A declaration of trust concerning land or any interest therein must be manifested and proved by some writing signed by some person who is able to declare the same or by his will.'

Example one

Claud is the owner of a house known as 'The Laurels' and says to some friends: 'From now on I am holding "The Laurels" in trust for my children Tom and Tim,' This is not enforceable, as there is nothing in writing.

Points to note:

- The actual declaration of trust need not be in writing. The words 'manifested and proved' require only written evidence of the details of the trust and do not require that the actual trust should be in writing. Therefore evidence can be, for example, in two or more documents which are linked.
- The signature of the settlor is probably needed. The words in s.53(1)(b) are 'signed by some person who is able to declare the same' and this is generally taken to mean that an agent cannot sign although the point has never been decided.

- The requirement in s.53(1)(b) applies only to express trusts and not to resulting, implied or constructive trusts (s.53 (2)). This exception is of great importance as it has enabled the courts to impose a resulting, implied or constructive trust in many cases where there was no written declaration of trust.

REVISION NOTE

Good examples of s.53(2) are those involving disputes over the beneficial entitlement to the family home and where it is felt necessary to impose a trust to prevent fraud or unconscionable conduct (see Chapter 9 and below).

- No formalities are required for *inter vivos* declarations of trusts of other property. Where the trust is created by will there are statutory requirements but these will not be relevant for a trusts exam as wills fall within the law of succession.

  Note the distinction between the formalities requirements and constitution of a trust (Chapter 6). Constitution deals with the actual transfer of the trust property but here we are concerned with a preliminary issue: Did the actual declaration of a trust observe the required formalities?

Failure to observe the requirements of s.53(1)(b)

Section 53(1)(b) itself is silent on the position when these requirements are not complied with but it is accepted that this will not make the trust void but only unenforceable (*Gardner* v. *Rowe* (1828)). *Void* means that the trust is of no effect at all. *Unenforceable* means that, although the trust is valid, it cannot be enforced in any legal proceedings.

However, in the case below, the court held that a trust could be imposed where the effect of the operation of s.53(1)(b) would be to permit fraud.

KEY CASE

***Rochefoucauld* v. *Boustead* [1897] 1 Ch 196 (CA)**

Concerning: whether a formality requirement should be set aside as it is an instrument of fraud

Facts

The claimant had mortgaged land but was having difficulty in repaying the mortgage. The defendant bought the land and orally agreed to hold it as trustee for the claimant. However, he treated the land as his own.

Legal principle

The claimant was entitled to an account of profits made on the land because although the trust was in the claimant's favour, not being in writing it did not satisfy the requirements of what is now s.53(1)(b), LPA 1925. It would thus be a fraud on the defendant's part to take the profits for himself.

FURTHER THINKING

This case is sometimes used as an example of the operation of constructive trusts as the 'instrument of fraud' principle is usually found in that context. You will gain marks for pointing out that here an express trust was imposed but you should point out that in other cases the courts have thought that a resulting or a constructive trust was more appropriate and, of course, these trusts are exempted from the formality requirement of s.53(1)(b) by s.53(2) (above). An instance of this is *Hodgson* v. *Marks* (1971) (see Chapter 8) and see also Chapter 9.

Dispositions of equitable interests arising under trusts

It is vital to be absolutely clear about when this happens by contrast with a declaration of trust which was dealt with above. One simple way is this:

- s.53(1)(b) applies when a trust is being declared.
- s.53(1)(c) applies when the trust is up and running but it is intended to move interests of beneficiaries under it (i.e. equitable interests) from one person to another.

Note that these two subsections operate at different stages (see Figure 5.1).

Figure 5.1

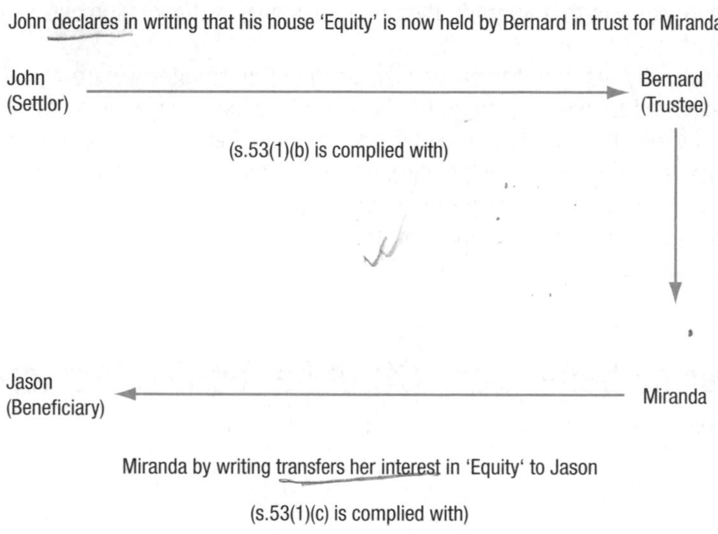
John declares in writing that his house 'Equity' is now held by Bernard in trust for Miranda
John
(Settlor)
Bernard
(Trustee)
(s.53(1)(b) is complied with)
Jason
(Beneficiary)
Miranda
Miranda by writing transfers her interest in 'Equity' to Jason
(s.53(1)(c) is complied with)

KEY STATUTE

Law of Property Act 1925, s.53(1)(c)

A disposition of an equitable interest or trust must be in writing signed either by the settlor or by his authorised agent.

Points to note:

- The actual disposition must be in writing. Written evidence will not suffice.
- The signature of an agent is sufficient.
- Section 53(1)(c) does not, by virtue of s.53(2), apply to resulting, implied or constructive trusts.
- Where a disposition of an equitable interest is made which is to be held on trust, then although the actual disposition must be in writing, the actual details of the trust need not be (*Re Tyler's Fund Trusts* (1967)).
- There is no requirement for the trustees to be notified of the disposition – a useful point to add in an exam answer.

Application of s.53(1)(c)

An exam question will deal with situations where the application of s.53(1)(c) has been considered by the courts. We will now look at each of these but before we do, you may find the following quote from Moffat (2005: 130) useful: 'if at the commencement of a transaction a person has a subsisting equitable interest and at the end no longer has that interest, then there has been a disposition within s.53(1)(c)'.

The reason why many of the cases discussed in this chapter were brought was that settlors have tried to avoid payment of stamp duty which is payable on the written instrument by which property is transferred, but many settlors have argued that as a particular transaction is not a disposition within the meaning of s.53(1)(c), no writing is needed and therefore no stamp duty is payable.

In the following examples, T holds on trust for X absolutely. T is the trustee and X is the beneficiary.

Transfer by beneficiary (X) of her equitable interest to another

Figure 5.2

X transfers her interest to Y
T
X
Y

In Figure 5.2 writing is obviously needed.

Direction to a beneficiary (X) to trustees that they are now to hold on trust for another person

Figure 5.3

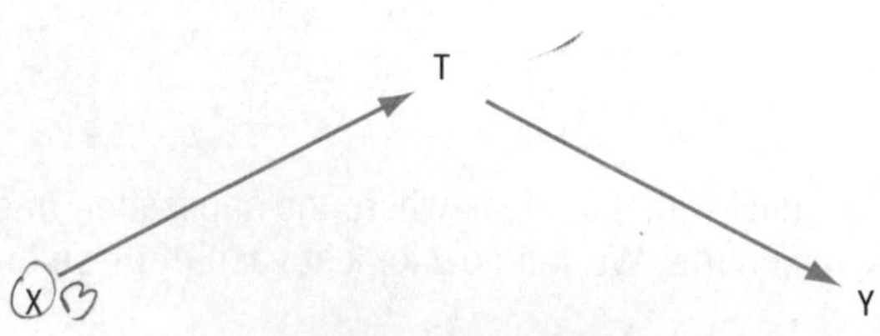
X directs T to hold the property on trust for Y
T
X
Y

Figure 5.3 shows an example.

KEY CASE

***Grey* v. *IRC* [1960] AC 1 (HL)**

Concerning: whether a direction by a beneficiary to trustees to hold the trust property on trust for another is a disposition within s.53 (1)(c)

Facts

The settlor transferred shares to trustees to hold as nominees for him. He then orally (i.e. no writing) directed the trustees to hold the shares on trust for his grandchildren and the trustees later executed a written declaration of trust.

Legal principle

A direction by a beneficiary to trustees to hold on trust for another is a disposition within s.53(1)(c).

Transfer of the legal estate by a bare trustee to another

KEY DEFINITION

A **bare trustee** is a trustee with no active duties and so can be given directions by the beneficiary to transfer the legal estate.

Example two

X (beneficiary) directs T to transfer shares to Y so that Y becomes the absolute owner. A possible form of words could be: 'All my interest in the shares is to go to Y.' The word 'all' could mean that not only the equitable interest in the shares, which belongs to X, but also the legal title to them, which is held by T, should go to Y.

KEY CASE

***Vandervell* v. *IRC* [1967] 2 AC 291 (HL)**

Concerning: whether a transfer of the legal estate, where there is an existing equitable interest, to another requires writing under s.53(1)(c)

Facts

A bank which held shares for Vandervell as a **bare trustee** transferred them, on his directions, to the Royal College of Surgeons subject to an option exercisable by Vandervell Trustees Ltd to repurchase the shares. The bank's legal title to the shares and Vandervell's equitable interest in them were accordingly both transferred and it was held that this transaction was not caught by s.53(1)(c) and so writing was not needed.

Legal principle

A transfer of the legal estate to another does not require writing.

Although the equitable interest passes from X to Y this is done automatically with the transfer of the legal estate and thus there is no separate disposition.

New trusts are declared by the trustee with the consent of the beneficiary

Example three

T declares, with the agreement of X, that he now holds the property on trust for W.

KEY CASE

***Re Vandervell's Trusts (No. 2)* [1974] Ch 269 (CA)**

Concerning: declaration of new trusts

Facts

Following from the decision in *Vandervell* v. *IRC* (above) Vandervell instructed Vandervell Trustees to exercise the option to repurchase the shares which were intended to be held on the trusts of the Vandervell children's settlement.

Legal principle

It was held that where new trusts are declared with the consent of the beneficiary then this was not within s.53(1)(c) so writing was not required.

FURTHER THINKING

See Green (1984).

Beneficiary contracts to transfer his equitable interest

Example four

X contracts with Z to transfer his interest under the trust to him.

The law here awaits clarification and the leading case is:

KEY CASE

***Oughtred* v. *IRC* [1960] AC 206 (HL)**

Concerning: whether a contract to transfer a beneficial interest under a trust is caught by s.53(1)(c)

Facts

X and Y had separate interests in shares in a private company. They orally agreed to exchange their interests and the IRC claimed stamp duty on the actual written transfer of the shares.

Legal principle

In the case of a contract to sell shares in a private company the remedy of specific performance is available because the shares are unique and so a constructive trust arises in favour of the buyer. The buyer does not acquire a full beneficial interest until the formal written transfer. This is therefore the disposition and s.53(1)(c) applies to it. Lord Radcliffe, however, dissented and held that Mrs Oughtred obtained the ownership in equity by virtue of the agreement and this view has been supported by later cases (see *Re Hay* [1982]).

FURTHER THINKING

Note that a later case to deal with the matter in depth, *Neville* v. *Wilson* [1997] supports Lord Radcliffe's argument (see Figure 5.4). See, for a discussion of this case, Milne (1997).

Figure 5.4

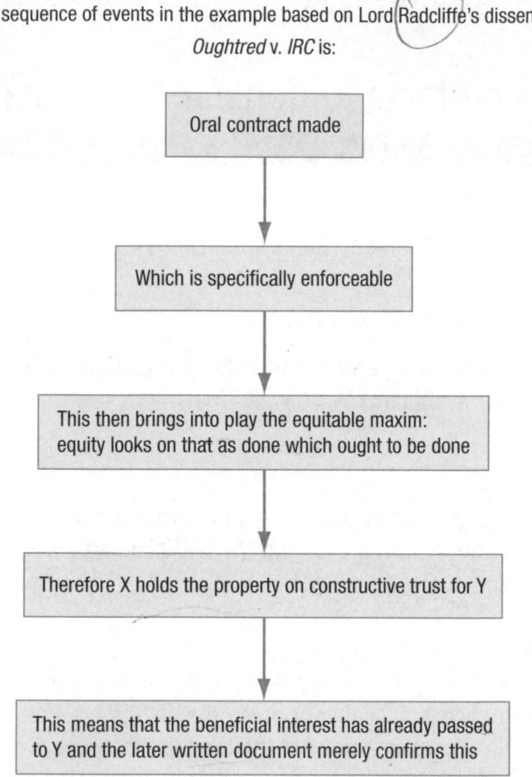
The sequence of events in the example based on Lord Radcliffe's dissent in
Oughtred v. *IRC* is:
Oral contract made
Which is specifically enforceable
This then brings into play the equitable maxim:
equity looks on that as done which ought to be done
Therefore X holds the property on constructive trust for Y
This means that the beneficial interest has already passed
to Y and the later written document merely confirms this

Beneficiary declares herself trustee

As a sub-trust has been created (Figure 5.5), it can be argued that this is a declaration of trust and so it falls within s.53(1)(b), in which case writing is only needed if it concerns land. However, if X has no active duties to perform and is thus a bare trustee then the effect is that X will have disappeared from the picture and there may be a disposition.

Figure 5.5

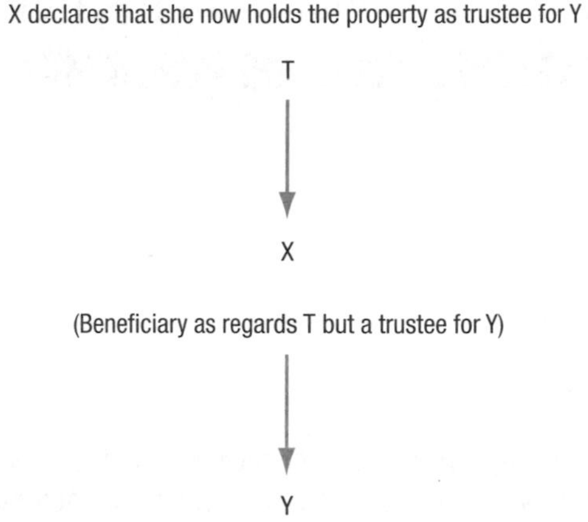

X declares that she now holds the property as trustee for Y

T

X

(Beneficiary as regards T but a trustee for Y)

Y

Beneficiary surrenders her equitable interest

Example five

X surrenders her interest to T1 and T2.

The position is uncertain but it could be argued, by analogy with *Vandervell* v. *IRC* (above) that as the legal and equitable titles are now merged there is no disposition.

Beneficiary disclaims her equitable interest

Example six

X, as soon as she becomes aware that she has an equitable interest, disclaims it.

KEY CASE

***Re Paradise Motor Co. Ltd* [1968] 1 WLR 1125 (HC)**

Concerning: disclaimer of an equitable interest

Facts

The facts were the same as in the example.

Legal principle

Writing is not needed here because 'a disclaimer operates by way of avoidance and not by way of disposition' (Danckwerts LJ).

Beneficiary under a staff pension fund appoints a nominee to receive benefits from the fund

Example seven

X, a beneficiary under a staff pension fund, appoints T to receive the money payable by the fund in the event of X's death.

KEY CASE

***Re Danish Bacon Co. Ltd Staff Pension Fund* [1971] 1 WLR 248 (HC)**

Concerning: nominations of benefits in a pension fund

Facts

An employee had nominated his wife to receive benefits payable to him under a pension fund and had then, by a separate letter, changed his mind.

Legal principle

Megarry J doubted if this was a disposition requiring writing, but, if it was, the writing was supplied by connecting the two documents.

Failure to comply with the requirements of S.53(1)(c)

The result is that the disposition is void.

Why formalities are needed

- To prevent fraud. This is the rationale for s.53(1)(c).

Example eight

John says that Susan has declared that she now holds her house on trust for him. Susan denies this. The only way in which John can prove this is by producing written evidence. This is the same principle as the requirement of writing in an actual contract for the sale of land.

- To enable the trustees to know what is going on. This is the rationale for s.53(1)(c).

Example nine

Gerald is a trustee of property for Jane. Jane tells Gerald that she has transferred her interest to Mark and in future Gerald should treat Mark as the beneficiary. What if

Jane is wrong? Gerald must require writing to prove that Jane's beneficial interest has been transferred to Mark (see below).

FURTHER THINKING

The complexity of this area has led to calls for reform. The Law Commission proposed to issue a Consultation Paper in 1999 which could have led to legislation but due to work on other projects it was put back and there is no date for any proposals. Look at Battersby (1979) for a critique of the law.

Chapter summary: Putting it all together

TEST YOURSELF

- [ ] Can you tick all the points from the **revision checklist** at the beginning of this chapter?
- [ ] Take the **end-of-chapter quiz** on the companion website.
- [ ] Test your knowledge of the cases with the **revision flashcards** on the website.
- [ ] Attempt the **essay question** from the beginning of this chapter using the guidelines below.
- [ ] Go to the companion website to try out **other questions**.

Answer guidelines

See the problem question at the start of this chapter.

A diagram illustrating how to structure your answer is available on the website.

Begin by explaining why Hubert's question is important. If Isabel has really divested herself of any interest in the property then it will no longer form part of her estate. Then look at each point in turn:

- The Gables: This appears to be an attempt to declare a trust of land but **your marks will be increased** if you discuss whether this is a declaration of trust anyway. Isabel has not actually used the word 'trust' here so you can make use of your knowledge of certainty of intention to create a trust (see Chapter 3).

  Assuming that it is a declaration of trust then does it comply with the requirements of s.53(1)(b) LPA 1925? Clearly not as it is not in writing or evidenced by writing. So the declaration is not void but cannot be enforced against Isabel's estate.
- £20,000 in the bank account: The same points apply here as well: is there an actual declaration of trust? If it is then it is valid as s.53(1)(b) only applies to land.
- Shares in the ABC Co.: Isabel is a beneficiary here and she is attempting to dispose of her equitable interest under the trust. Again, extra marks for spotting that she has not actually used the words 'dispose of my equitable interest' but this is what she has actually done. Refer to s.53(1)(c) and note that it requires writing. This case is similar to *Grey* v. *IRC* in that the beneficiary has directed the trustee to hold the property for another rather than make a direct disposition but applying *Grey* v. *IRC* it is still caught by s.53(1)(c). Therefore as she has not used writing it is void and so Isabel's estate is still a beneficiary of the shares.

Make your answer stand out

Show that you have:

- a thorough knowledge of the law which is clearly applied
- paid close attention to the actual words of the relevant sections of the LPA
- knowledge of the reasons why formalities are required – a mention of this would impress the examiner in an answer to a problem question.

FURTHER READING

Battersby, G. (1979) 'Formalities for the Disposition of Equitable Interests under Trusts', 43 *Conv.* 17 at 38.

Green, B. (1984) 'Grey, Oughtred and Vandervell – A Contextual Re Appraisal', 47 MLR 385.

Milne, P. (1997) 'Oughtred Revisted', 113 LQR 213.

Moffat, G. (2005) *Trusts Laws and Materials*, p. 130, 4th edition, Cambridge: Cambridge University Press.

Nolan, R. (1996) 'The Triumph of Technicality', 55 CLJ 436.

6 Constitution

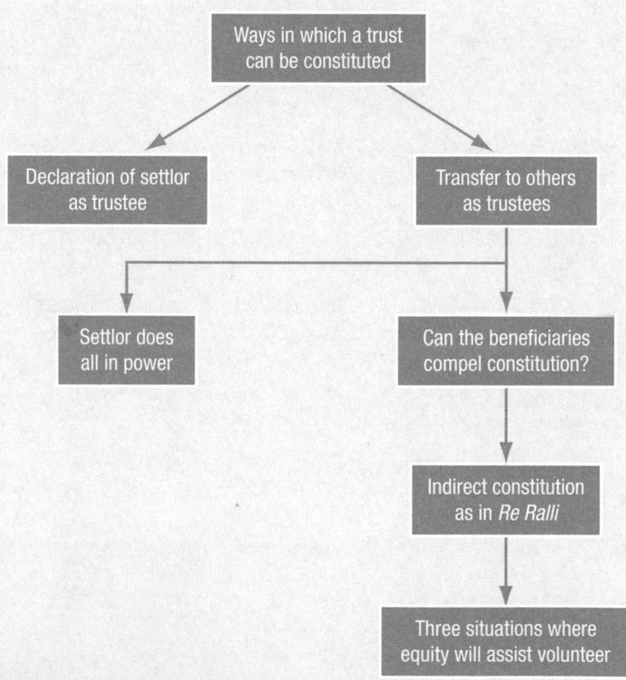

A printable version of this topic map is available from www.pearsoned.co.uk/lawexpress

Revision Checklist

Essential points you should know:

- [ ] the methods of constituting a trust
- [ ] the principle in *Re Rose* and its application in more recent cases
- [ ] the position of beneficiaries and trustees where the trust is incompletely constituted
- [ ] indirect constitution as in *Re Ralli*
- [ ] the three ways in which equity may assist a volunteer.

Introduction: Understanding constitution

Constitution of trusts is one of the major areas of equity and trusts and is likely to attract a question.

It can be one on its own or the question can be combined with either or both certainties or formalities and so you should always revise these areas carefully. There have been two recent cases, *Choithram (T) International SA* v. *Pagarani* [2001] and *Pennington* v. *Waine* [2002] which are obviously likely to inspire questions. Note that two topics may only be dealt with in outline in an equity course as they may appear in other subjects: *Donationes mortis causa* (succession) and *Estoppel* (land law).

Assessment advice

Essay questions

A familiar essay question asks you to comment on the equitable maxim 'equity will not assist a volunteer' in the light of the law on constitution. Another could ask about the effect of *Pennington* v. *Waine* [2002] on the requirements for constitution or deal with particular areas such as the three cases where equity may assist a volunteer.

Problem questions

Problem questions often involve a range of situations and ask you to decide if the trust has been completely constituted in each. This is a good area for picking up marks as there will be a wide range of issues and you ought to be able to say

Assessment advice

something useful on at least some of them! In many questions the person attempting the transfer (X) will have died and so the contest will be between the trustee/beneficiary who will be claiming that the trust was properly constituted and the person (Y) who was left the property under the will of X. Y will of course claim that the trust was incompletely constituted and so it still formed part of X's estate when he died and so passes to them. Do make a note of who Y is at the start of your answer and, as ever, always find a home for the property: do not leave it unallocated.

When answering a problem question identify, in relation to each piece of property, what formalities were required to validly transfer it and if they have been complied with. If not, then consider if any of the exceptions outlined below apply.

Sample question

Could you answer this question? Below is a typical problem question that could arise on this topic. Guidelines on answering the question are included at the end of this chapter, whilst a sample essay question and guidance on tackling it can be found on the companion website.

Problem question

Joshua suffered a haemorrhage and was rushed to hospital. His niece, Belinda, his son, Charles, his daughter, Fiona, and his friend, Laura, all visited him.

He said to Belinda: 'Here are the deeds to my house "Laurels". As you know, I have always intended you to have it and now it is yours.'

He asked Charles to bring him the lease to his shop and he wrote on It: ' I now declare that the benefit of this shop belongs to Charles absolutely.'

He told Fiona: 'You have been wonderful to me. You gave up your job to look after me and it was always understood between us that you would be rewarded. My seaside cottage is now yours.'

He said to Laura: 'I am not long for this world. Here is my post office savings book. This account is now yours. I have made out the necessary forms to put it into your name – here they are.'

That night Joshua died when the hospital was struck by lightning. His will appointed Fiona as his executrix.

Can you advise Belinda, Charles, Fiona and Laura as to any claims they might have to Joshua's property? Would it make any difference to your answer if Joshua had died six months later when playing tennis from an undetected heart condition?

Ways in which a trust can be constituted

REVISION NOTE

Before looking at constitution, note the distinction between constitution and formalities, which were dealt with in Chapter 5. Questions may deal with both of these.

Look at these situations:

Example one

Situation one	Situation two
Fred transfers £1000 into a trust account in the name of his two trustees (Tim and Ted) to be held on the terms of a trust which he has declared for his two children, Mark and Charlotte.	Fred promises Tim and Ted that he will transfer £1000 into the trust account for Mark and Charlotte but fails to do so.

The difference is obvious: in the first situation Fred has transferred the money into the names of his trustees and so it is no longer Fred's money; in the second Fred has promised to do so but no transfer has taken place.

In situation one the trust is said to be constituted but in situation two it is not.

KEY DEFINITIONS

A trust is **constituted** when the legal title to the trust property is vested in the trustee(s).

A trust is **unconstituted** when the legal title to the trust property is not vested in the trustee(s).

EXAM TIP

Always begin your answer to a problem question on constitution by identifying whether constitution has taken place. It almost certainly will not have done so and so you will then be able to continue by deciding if there is any way in which the trust can be **constituted**.

Take situation two. The trust has not been constituted. What, if anything, can Mark and Charlotte do?

Your starting point must be the maxim that 'Equity will not assist a volunteer' (e.g. see Lord Eldon in *Ellison* v. *Ellison* (1802)).

KEY DEFINITION

A **volunteer** is a person who has not provided any consideration for a promise.

(Note that in equity the term consideration is wider than in the common law of contract.)

Are Mark and Charlotte volunteers? Yes, as there is no evidence of their having provided consideration for Fred's promise to transfer £1000 to Tim and Tom for their benefit.

The point that equity will not assist volunteers is not the end of the matter but is a good and clear way to start!

Methods of constituting a trust

Figure 6.1

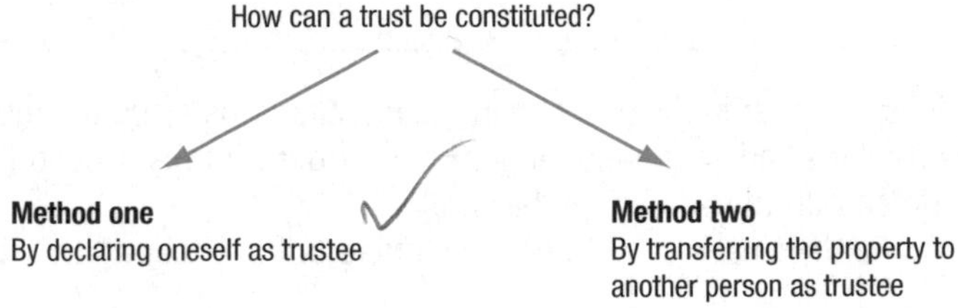

The authority for the two methods shown in Figure 6.1 is in the judgment of Turner LJ in *Milroy v. Lord* (1862).

We will deal with Method one now so as to concentrate on Method two later.

Method one: declaration of settlor as trustee

Example two

Jason has £1000 in a bank account and says to his son, Christopher: 'I am now the trustee of this money for you.'

The effect is that a trust has been set up with Jason as trustee and Christopher as beneficiary (see Figure 6.2).

Figure 6.2

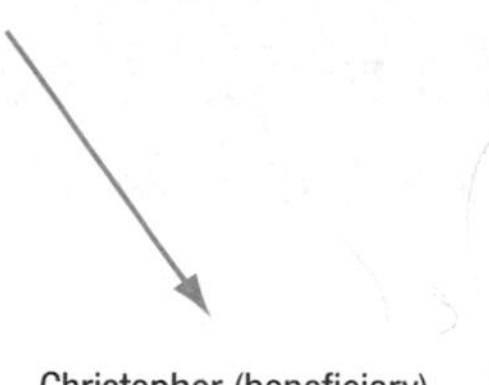

However, exam questions do not make the scenario as simple as this!

There have been a number of cases on this point and you should note the following carefully:

- *Jones* v. *Lock* (1865)
- *Richards* v. *Delbridge* (1874)
- *Paul* v. *Constance* (1977).

In all of these cases the issue was whether words used by the settlor were enough to make him/her a trustee.

REVISION NOTE

Go back to Chapter 3 and revise intention to create a trust.

The most recent case is as follows:

KEY CASE

***Choithram (T) International SA* v. *Pagarani* [2001] 2 All ER 492 (PC)**

Concerning: declaration of self as trustee

Facts

X executed a trust deed which set up a charitable foundation and then said: 'I now give all my wealth to the foundation' (or words to this effect).

Legal principle

This was sufficient to constitute the trust as A was one of the trustees of the foundation and it did not matter that the property had not been vested in the other trustees. In addition, although the words used looked like an outright gift they must have meant that X was constituting a trust.

FURTHER THINKING

Read Hopkins (2001) or Clarke (2001) on this case.

Method two: transfer to others as trustees

Here there must be three parties (see Figure 6.3).

Figure 6.3

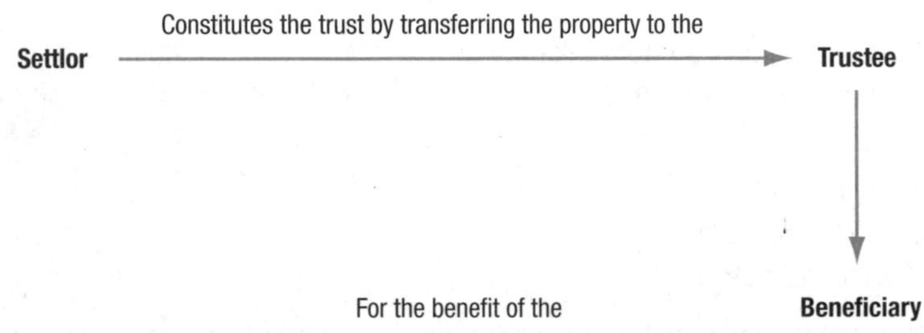

Example three

Take example two above. Suppose that Jason had declared himself a trustee, not of £1000 in his bank account, but of his house.

This is Method one and as this is freehold land, one formality would be needed:

1 The actual declaration of trust would need to be in writing (s.53(1)(b), LPA 1925 and see Chapter 3).

Suppose that Method two was used and the scenario was:

Example four

Jason intends to transfer his house to Edith to hold on trust for Christopher.

We would now need two formalities:

1 As above, s.53(1)(b), LPA must be complied with.
2 Section 52(1), LPA which requires transfers of freehold land to be by deed.

Settlor does all in power to constitute the trust (i.e. to transfer the property to the trustees)

Example five

Anne is the owner of 5000 shares in Midland Optical Illusion Co. Ltd, a private company. She wishes to transfer them to her daughter, Susan. However, a private company can refuse to register a transfer.

KEY CASE

Re Rose **[1952] Ch 499 (HC)**

Concerning: what is needed for the settlor to do all in his power to make the transfer?

Facts

The settlor executed a deed transferring shares in a private company to trustees.

Legal principle

It was enough if the settlor had done everything in his power to make the transfer binding and this was when the deed was executed. Although directors of a private company have a discretion to refuse to register a transfer, at the moment when the deed was executed the settlor had done all in his power to make the transaction binding on him.

This was applied in *Mascall* v. *Mascall* (1985) to a transfer of registered land: here it is the Land Registry who completes the transfer.

KEY CASE

Pennington **v.** ***Waine*** **[2002] EWCA Civ 227**

Concerning: what is needed to make a transfer binding on a person when another person or body needs to complete the transfer?

Facts

A donor had executed a form transferring shares in a private company to her nephew but had not delivered it to him, instead it had gone to the auditor of the company. The gift was completed, as it was not necessary for the form to be delivered to the nephew.

Legal principle

A gift can be deemed to be complete if it would have been unconscionable for the donor to change their mind at this point.

FURTHER THINKING

This case, like *Choithram* (above) is seen as a controversial relaxation of the rules on constitution as the donor did not do all in her power to complete the transfer. Read more on it: see Clarke (2002) and Garton (2003).

Other formal requirements for transfer of property

Other property requires other formalities to transfer it: equitable interests need writing (s.53(1)(c), LPA 1925; see Chapter 3); and chattels need a deed of gift or the intention to give them or parting with possessions, and shares need the appropriate transfer form and registration of the transferee as owner.

Can the beneficiaries compel constitution?

Equity will not assist a volunteer. A volunteer is a person who has not provided consideration. So if the beneficiaries have not provided consideration then equity will not assist them unless the situation is within the three exceptional situations dealt with below. It then becomes crucial to know what is meant by consideration.

Consideration in equity has a wider meaning than at common law because equity also includes marriage consideration.

KEY DEFINITION

Marriage consideration includes the husband and wife and the issue of the marriage.

Marriage consideration will appear when a settlement is made either before or after marriage and (this is the crucial point) in consideration of marriage, under which the settlor promises to settle property on his or her (future) husband or wife. If so, they can enforce the promise if it is not carried out and so can their issue (see *Pullan* v. *Koe* (1913).

Suppose that the beneficiaries have not given consideration but they are parties to a deed of covenant under which there is a promise to constitute a trust by settling property on them?

Note that:

- Equity recognises marriage consideration. Common law does not.
- Common law recognises promises made in a deed (*Cannon* v. *Hartley* (1949)). Equity does not.
- Common law remedy is damages. Equitable remedy will probably be specific performance.

In addition the Contracts (Rights of Third Parties) Act 1999 may change the answer.

Take some examples and see how these principles apply to them. Note that for now we are considering whether the beneficiary is able to enforce the promise. We will consider the position of the trustee later.

Assume for now that the Contracts (Rights of Third Parties) Act 1999 does not apply.

Example six

John promises his fiancée Miranda that, in contemplation of his marriage to her he will transfer £10,000 to Robert to hold on trust for her. He fails to do so.

Can Miranda enforce this promise?	Yes
In equity or common law?	Equity – marriage consideration

Therefore equitable remedies, e.g. specific performance (SP).

Example seven

John promises Miranda, his girlfriend, that he will transfer £10,000 to Robert on trust for her but fails to do so.

Can Miranda enforce this promise?	No

Miranda is a volunteer – unlike in Example six there is no evidence of marriage consideration.

Example eight

John promises Miranda by a deed to which John, Miranda and Robert are parties that he will transfer £10,000 to Robert to hold on trust for her but fails to do so.

Can Miranda enforce the promise?	Not in equity

Equity does not enforce promises in a deed made without consideration – example of the maxim that equity does not assist a volunteer – Miranda has given no consideration.

However, common law will give a remedy for broken promises in a deed – so Miranda can claim damages.

KEY STATUTES

Contracts (Rights of Third Parties) Act 1999, s.1

Section 1 enables a person who is not a party to a contract to take the benefit of a contractual term in two cases:

1 If the contract expressly provides that they may do so.
2 If a term of the contract purports to confer a benefit, unless on a proper construction of the term it appears that it was not intended to be enforceable by the third party.

How could this affect the above situations?

- It only applies to contracts made on or after 11 May 2000.
- It will allow an action by a beneficiary where the contract or deed (the Act includes deeds – s.7(3)), between the settlor and the trustee expressly conferred a benefit on the beneficiary.

This means that provided there was a contract and not just a promise a beneficiary may be able to enforce the obligation to constitute a trust in their favour. So the answer to Example six may be different and in Example seven the volunteer might be able to sue under this Act as well as at common law, although there is doubt as to whether specific performance can be obtained under the Act.

Trustees' position where trust is incompletely constituted

What of Robert, the trustee in the above examples? Assuming that Miranda is unable to take action herself, can he do so on her behalf? The answer is probably no, although the cases do not give a definite answer: see, for example, *Re Pryce* [1917]; *Re Kay* [1939]; *Re Cook's Settlement Trusts* [1965].

Indirect constitution of a trust

KEY CASE

Re Ralli's Will Trust **[1964] Ch 288 (HC)**

Concerning: indirect constitution of a trust

Facts

(Simplified) The Trustee was also the executor under the will of the settlor/testator and the trust was held to be constituted.

Legal principle

A trust can be constituted if the trust property reaches the intended trustee in an indirect way (i.e. as in the above case where the trustee was also the executor) and one which was not intended by the settlor.

EXAM TIP

If the scenario has the same person as both the trustee under an unconstituted trust and as the executor under the settlor's will then look carefully to see if *Re Ralli* applies. This makes it easy to spot in an exam.

Three ways in which equity may assist a volunteer

EXAM TIP

These are exceptions to the principle that 'equity will not assist a volunteer'. Note that they deal with gifts but they can also be relevant to attempts to constitute a trust.

1. Rule in *Strong* v. *Bird*

KEY CASE

***Strong* v. *Bird* (1874) LR 18 Eq 315 (CA)**

Concerning: perfecting an incomplete gift (i.e. one which has been promised but not made)

Facts

X had borrowed £1100 from his stepmother but did not repay £900 of it. Her will appointed him as her executor.

Legal principle

Where there is an intention to make an immediate gift, or to release a debt, and that intention continues until the death then the appointment of the donee as executor perfects the gift/releases the debt. Therefore the debt of £900 owed by X to his stepmother was released.

Example nine

Pam promises Teresa that she will give Teresa her car. Pam then appoints Teresa her executor. On Pam's death Teresa can claim the car.

Suppose that before her death Pam had told her daughter, Sophie, that she could borrow the car. Here the rule in *Strong* v. *Bird* would not apply as there needs to be a continuing intention to make an immediate gift (*Re Gonin* (1979)) and clearly this cannot now be the case.

Does this rule also apply to administrators appointed under intestacy? See *Re Gonin* (1979) (a very useful case for exams).

2. *Donatio mortis causa* (DMC)

This exception applies where a gift is made:

- in contemplation of death
- where the subject matter of the gift, or the means of control of it, or some essential indication of title, was delivered to the donee
- where there was an intention to make the gift conditional on death.

This topic is generally easy enough provided that you learn the above rules and the relevant case law.

One particularly important case is as follows:

KEY CASE

***Sen* v. *Hedley* [1991] Ch 425 (CA)**

Concerning: whether land can be the subject of a DMC

Facts

The deceased was terminally ill and said to the claimant (a very close friend for many years): 'The house is yours, Margaret. You have the keys. They are in your bag. The deeds are in a steel box.'

Legal principle

There can be a valid DMC of land and there was a valid DMC here as all the requirements were satisfied.

REVISION NOTE

The effect of a DMC is that pending the death of the donor the property is held on a constructive trust for the donee (see *Sen* v. *Hedley*). Check Chapter 9 and make sure that you are clear what a constructive trust is.

3. Estoppel

Estoppel is a principle which also appears in land law but it may arise here in the context of incomplete gifts. Although some aspects of the principle are subject to debate the definition below is a good starting point:

KEY DEFINITION

Estoppel arises where one person (the representee) has been led to act on the representation of another (the representor). If so, and if the representee then acts to their detriment on the basis of this promise, then in equity the court may grant the representee a remedy.

KEY CASE

***Gillett* v. *Holt* [2001] Ch 210 (CA)**

Concerning: estoppel

Facts

Holt promised Gillett on several occasions that he would leave him his farm in his will and, on the basis of this, Gillett worked as Holt's farm manager at a lower wage than he could have received elsewhere.

Legal principle

Holt was estopped from going back on his promise. As he had now made a will leaving the farm to another (X) the court directed that on Holt's death the farm was to be held on trust by X for Gillett.

Note also *Thorner* v. *Curtis* (2007) – a recent example of **estoppel**. Inclusion of recent cases in exam answers should improve your marks! Look at *Jennings* v. *Rice* (2002) on the exercise of the court's discretion on what remedy is needed to satisfy the estoppel. Always mention this in an answer on estoppel.

Chapter summary: **Putting it all together**

TEST YOURSELF

- ☐ Can you tick all the points from the **revision checklist** at the beginning of this chapter?
- ☐ Take the **end-of-chapter quiz** on the companion website.
- ☐ Test your knowledge of the cases with the **revision flashcards** on the website.
- ☐ Attempt the **essay question** from the beginning of this chapter using the guidelines below.
- ☐ Go to the companion website to try out **other questions**.

Answer guidelines

See the problem question at the start of the chapter.

Valid transfers by John? Check formalities. If not, DMC? Estoppel? Note Fiona is executor.

- **Belinda:** No valid transfer. Here involved and LPA 1925, s.52(1) must be complied with – deed required and no deed. Could be a DMC – note *Sen* v. *Hedley* can have a DMC of land – but it appears to be an outright gift and not one conditional on death. Therefore it fails and the property remains in Joshua's estate.
- **Charles:** Is this a declaration that Joshua now holds on trust for Charles? Older cases may be against this (e.g. see *Richards* v. *Delbridge*) but note the more relaxed view taken in *Choithram*. If it is not a valid declaration of trust then the property forms part of Joshua's estate.
- **Fiona:** Possibility of a DMC but there is no delivery of any indication of title. Could be estoppel: set out the requirements for a valid estoppel but do not come to a definite conclusion – evidence not enough to decide.
- **Laura:** Could be a DMC but again looks like an outright gift. Apply *Pennington* v. *Waine* and *Re Rose* and see if could be valid on the principle that Joshua has done all that he can to transfer title to the property.
- If Fiona is appointed executrix then the gift to her is perfected – *Strong* v. *Bird*.
- If Joshua died six months later when playing tennis then he must have recovered from his original illness and so, if there were any valid DMCs they would have been revoked.

Make your answer stand out

This answer used the recent cases of *Choithram* and *Pennington* but you will gain extra marks if you can show how the approach in earlier cases differed. In addition, the judges in the Court of Appeal in *Pennington* gave different reasons for their decisions; look at these and discuss them.

FURTHER READING

Clarke, P. (2001) All ER Review 265.
Clarke, P. (2002) All ER Review 229.
Gardner, S. (2006) 'The Remedial Discretion in Proprietary Estoppel – Again', 122 LQR 492.
Garton, J. (2003) 'The role of the trust mechanism in the Rule in Re Rose', 87 Conv. 364.
Halliwell, M. (2003) 'Perfecting imperfect gifts and trusts: have we reached the end of the Chancellor's foot?', 87 Conv. 192.
Hopkins, J. (2001) *Constitution of Trusts – A Novel Point*, 60 CLJ 483.

7 Secret and half-secret trusts

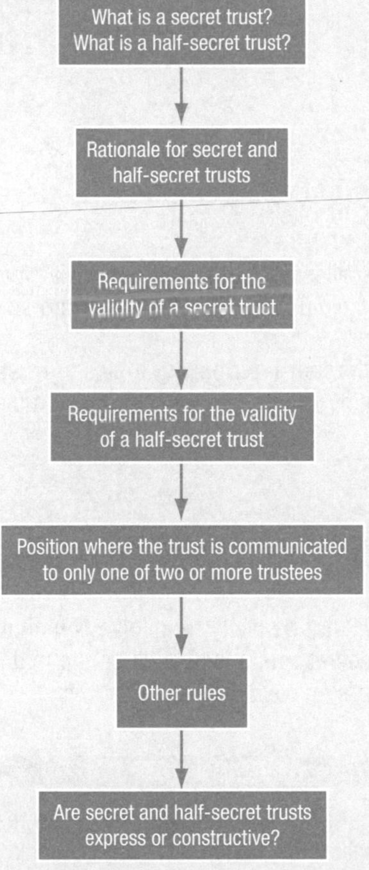

A printable version of this topic map is available from www.pearsoned.co.uk/lawexpress

Revision Checklist

Essential points you should know:

- [ ] the distinction between secret and half-secret trusts
- [ ] why equity enforces secret and half-secret trusts
- [ ] the requirements for the validity of secret and half-secret trusts.
- [ ] the importance of knowing whether these trusts are express or constructive
- [ ] the rules on what happens to the property when either of these trusts fail.

Introduction: **Understanding secret and half-secret trusts**

There is often a problem question on these trusts.

In addition, this topic is an excellent illustration of a familiar maxim of equity: *equity will not allow a statute to be used as an engine of fraud* and so it is useful for essay questions.

Secret trusts form one of the four interlocking topics in trusts law and you should be prepared for a question to involve one or more of these topics. A reminder of what they are:

- three certainties
- formalities
- secret trusts
- constitution.

A question on secret trusts will not be likely to involve constitution but it could well involve the others. If so, the secret trusts issue will be the main one but you will be expected to deal with the others as well.

REVISION NOTE

Where land is the subject matter of the intended trust then there is also a formality issue. Precisely what is explained later but go back to Chapter 5 now and revise formalities.

Assessment advice

Essay questions

An essay question on secret and half-secret trusts could involve either:

(a) a question on the theoretical basis of these trusts, or
(b) a question based on one of the maxims: equity will not allow a statute to be used as an instrument of fraud (the statute here is the Wills Act 1837) or equity looks to the intent rather than the form, i.e. equity looks at the intention to create a trust rather than whether the formalities have been complied with – here those in the Wills Act 1837.

The moral is to think clearly about just why these trusts should be enforced and be able to weigh up the opposing arguments.

Problem questions

Problems will require you to say if the trust is valid and so you must be able to apply the tests for the validity of a secret and half-secret trust. Almost certainly the problem will involve one or both of the decisions in *Re Keen* [1937] and *Re Stead* [1900] and, if you decide that the trust is valid, there will be subsidiary points to watch for: for example, did trustees/beneficiaries witness the will? Is it a trust of land? You will also need to bear in mind the requirements of certainty, as explained above.

Sample question

Can you answer this question? Below is a typical problem question that could arise on this topic. Guidelines on answering the question are included at the end of the chapter whilst a sample essay question and guidance on tackling it can be found on the companion website.

Problem question

Jennifer is aged 87 and had been told by her doctor that she may not have long to live. She has substantial savings, together with her house, 'The Laurels', which she does not wish to leave to any of her family, whom she dislikes, and so she explains the problem to her friends Mabel and Fanny. She tells them both that she intends to make them beneficiaries under her will but that she will let them know what to do with their bequests later. They are both puzzled but agree to help if they can. Jennifer telephones Mabel later that day and they have a long conversation.

Jennifer executes her will on 1 February, three days after she had spoken to Mabel and Fanny. In it, she leaves £50,000 and 'The Laurels' to Mabel to be used for 'the purposes which we have discussed' and £100,000 to Fanny. Mabel and Fanny were witnesses to the will. The local hospital is named as the residuary beneficiary.

Later that day, Jennifer gave Mabel an envelope with the words written on it: 'This contains important instructions. Open immediately on my death but not before.'

On 3 February Jennifer wrote to Fanny and told her that of the £100,000, £90,000 should be held on trust for all the employees and their relatives of Barset College to be distributed among them at Fanny's discretion. The other £10,000 is a gift to Fanny in memory of the good times that she and Jennifer shared together. Fanny received this letter on 4 February.

Jennifer died on 5 February. Mabel found that 'The Laurels' is to be held on trust for Alf, Jennifer's son, and the £50,000 is to be held on trust for Jack, an old friend of Jennifer. However, Jack predeceased Jennifer.

Advise Mabel and Fanny on whether the trusts are valid and, if not, for whose benefit the property should be held.

The distinction between secret and half-secret trusts

Example one	Example two
John wishes to leave £10,000 to his girlfriend Fifi but does not want his wife to know of this, as she is unaware of his relationship with Fifi. Accordingly, he decides to leave the property to someone who will hold it on trust to carry out his wishes.	Susan wishes to make a will as she is going into hospital for a major operation but she cannot decide who to leave her property to.
John's will reads: 'I leave £10,000 to Steve'.	Susan's will reads: 'I leave all my property to Deborah on the trusts which I have declared to her.'
This is a **secret trust** as the will does not disclose either the existence or the details of the trust. Ask the question; on reading the will, would anyone know that there was a trust? If not, the trust is secret.	This is a **half-secret trust** as, although the will discloses the existence of a trust it does not disclose the details of it.

EXAM TIP

If you are faced with a problem question on secret trusts in the exam, first look at the words of the will, as these will tell you if the trust is secret or half-secret. The rules for them are different in some respects and so it is vital to be clear at the outset which category the trust falls into.

EXAM TIP

The words used by the settlor should be looked at carefully to see that certainty of intention to create a trust is disclosed (e.g. in the will). If there is, then the trust will be half-secret.

If you are in doubt whether the words disclose a secret or a half-secret trust you should answer for both although it may be that the court would decide that there was enough evidence of an obligation for there to be a half-secret trust. In *Blackwell* v. *Blackwell* [1929] the will used the word 'purposes'.

Rationale for secret and half-secret trusts

The fraud rationale

This is that secret trusts must be enforced by equity to prevent fraud.

FURTHER THINKING

Look at the judgment of Lord Westbury in *McCormick* v. *Grogan* (1869) for a clear statement of the fraud rationale.

EXAM TIP

Secret trusts are excellent examples of the maxim 'equity will not allow a statute to be used as an engine of fraud' and an essay question may ask you to discuss this maxim. Make a list of examples of this maxim, and others that you come across, to be cited in answers. See Chapters 5 and 9 for further examples.

The intention rationale

This is that equity enforces half-secret trusts to give effect to the intentions of the settlor.

FURTHER THINKING

See the judgment of Lord Buckmaster in *Blackwell* v. *Blackwell* [1929] for a clear statement of the intention rationale.

EXAM TIP

Secret trusts normally arise in the context of gifts by will and these form the main part of this chapter. They can also arise when an *inter vivos* gift is made. An exam question will almost certainly involve gifts by will but an answer to an essay question will be improved by a discussion of secret trusts arising *inter vivos*.

Requirements for the validity of a secret trust

The requirements are as follows:

- the **intention** of the testator to create a trust (together with the trust property being certain and the objects of the trust satisfying the test for certainty of objects)
- **communication** of that intention to the intended trustees in the lifetime of the testator
- **acceptance** of the trust by the intended trustees either expressly or by acquiescence.

See *Ottaway* v. *Norman* [1972] where these were clearly stated.

Intention, subject matter and objects.

We saw above that certainty of intention is relevant in deciding whether the trust was secret or half-secret. In addition, all the three certainties must be present for both secret and half-secret trusts. It is possible, however, that there may be a doubt over this.

Suppose that Susan's will said: 'I leave all my property to Deborah for the purposes which I have indicated to her.' This may look like a secret trust at first sight but the words 'purposes which I have indicated to her' do not clearly disclose the existence of a trust. Your knowledge of the rules on certainty of intention will be needed here.

In *Marguilies* v. *Marguilies* (2000) a possible intended secret trust failed as there was a lack of certainty of intention. Compare the words used with those in *Gold* v. *Hill* (1998) where there was sufficient intention.

Communication

EXAM TIP

Always check that you have found a home for the property! If there is no valid trust decide where it will go. Where the secret trust was not communicated then it will be a gift to the intended trustee (donee).

KEY CASE

***Wallgrave* v. *Tebbs* (1855) 2 K & J 313 (HC)**

Concerning: communication of secret trusts

The facts of this case do not aid an understanding of the legal principle.

Legal principle

In cases of secret trusts the trust must be communicated during the lifetime of the testator so here the intended trustee took the property absolutely, as there was no trust.

Communication will be valid where the testator delivers a sealed envelope to the intended trustee with the direction: 'Not to be opened until after my death.' (*Re Keen* [1937].) However, the intended trustee must know that the envelope contains details of the trust and it must be handed to her during the lifetime of the testator.

A halfway situation

The testator tells the intended trustee that she is to hold the property on trust but does not communicate the details of the trust. Here the intended trustee cannot take the property beneficially, as she knows that she is a trustee and so she holds it on a resulting trust for the testator's estate (*Re Boyes* [1884]).

Acceptance

The intended trustee must accept the trust either expressly or by acquiescence and so silence will be enough for acceptance – contrast the position in contract. In *Moss* v. *Cooper* (1861) Wood VC referred to: 'Acquiescence either by words of consent or silence.'

Requirements for the validity of a half-secret trust

EXAM TIP

The only difference between the requirements for the validity of a half-secret trust and a secret trust is the rules on communication. Thus you already know two of the three requirements.

In the case of half-secret trusts intention to create a trust will appear (or not appear) in the will itself.

EXAM TIP

An exam question may not clearly indicate if the trust is secret or half-secret. In the exam question the words were 'for the purposes which we have discussed'. The word 'trust' was not mentioned but the word 'purposes' probably indicates a trust but may not. So you will gain extra marks by answering on the basis that it is half-secret (which it probably is) and then secret (which it might just be).

Communication in half-secret trusts

This is a favourite area for exam questions because the law is uncertain. There are two possible rules:

- **Rule one** (which is probably the law): Communication must be before the date of the execution of the will (*Re Keen*).

If this is the rule then the difference between the two types of trusts can be seen in Figure 7.1.

Figure 7.1

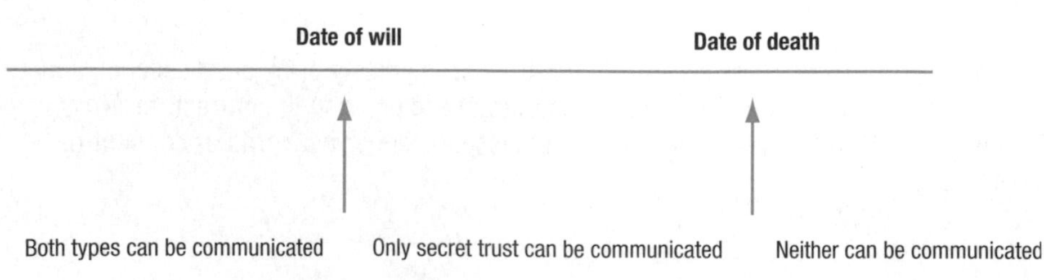

- **Rule two**: If the will states a time of communication then the trust must be communicated at that time. This rule also arises from *Re Keen* and the fact that there are two rules arises from the judgment of Lord Wright in *Re Keen*.

KEY CASE

***Re Keen* [1937] Ch 236 (CA)**

Concerning: communication of a half-secret trust

Facts

The testator left £10,000 to trustees to hold on trust and to be disposed of by them among such persons, etc. as may 'be notified by me to them during my lifetime'.

Legal principle

- The words 'to be notified by me' indicated an intention to make future communications and this was invalid as communication must be before the will.
- The actual communication was before the will and this conflicted with the words to 'be notified'.

A final point is that where a codicil is later added to a will this 'republishes the will' so that the date of the will is now the date of the codicil. This can affect the rules on communication:

Example three

Date of will: 1 January
Date of communication: 1 February
Communication is too late if Rule one is applied.
Date of Codicil: 1 March
Therefore:
Date of will now 1 March
Therefore communication valid.

Where the half-secret trust is not validly communicated the property is held on a resulting trust for the beneficiaries (e.g. the hospital in the exam question).

Position where the trust is communicated to only one of two or more trustees

KEY CASE

Re Stead **[1900] 1 Ch 237 (HC)**

Concerning: communication of a secret trust to some but not all intended trustees

The facts of this case do not aid an understanding of the legal principle.

Legal principle

- Where communication is to one of two joint tenants and this takes place before the will then all joint tenants are bound.
- Where communication is to one of two joint tenants after the will then only the one to whom the trust is communicated is bound.
- Where communication is to one of two tenants in common then only the one to whom the trust is communicated is bound.

Example four

Jason leaves £10,000 to Mark and Anthony. Before Jason executed the will he told Mark, but not Anthony, that he wanted the £10,000 to be held for the benefit of his daughter, Mary.

Mark and Anthony are joint tenants, as there are no words of severance, and so they are both bound. If the gift had been to Mark and Anthony in equal shares then they would have been tenants in common and so only Mark would have been bound. He would hold £5,000 on trust for Mary and Anthony would take the other £5,000 beneficially.

EXAM TIP

It is unlikely that the distinction between tenants in common and joint tenants will involve you learning fine points of distinction between them. Look for words of severance: if they are there the gift is to tenants in common, if they are not there the gift is to joint tenants.

FURTHER THINKING

This rule has been criticised (e.g. by Perrins (1972)).

EXAM TIP

For extra marks learn why this rule is felt to be unsatisfactory and what might replace it.

Other rules

These are as follows:

- Where there is an addition to the trust this must be communicated, e.g. if an additional sum is to be held on trust (*Re Colin Cooper* [1939]).
- Where a beneficiary under a secret trust witnesses the will this does not affect the gift as the trust is outside (dehors) the will (*Re Young)* [1951].
- Where a person is named as trustee in a half-secret trust and also witnesses it this will not affect the trust as they are not named as a beneficiary but a trustee.
- Where a person is a trustee under a secret trust and witnesses the will then they cannot take the property as they appear in the will to be beneficiaries.
- Where a beneficiary under a secret or half-secret trust dies before the testator the gift does not lapse but passes to their estate (*Re Gardner* [1920]). Had the gift been in a will then in most cases the gift would have lapsed.
- There is doubt as to whether a person can bring evidence to show that they were intended to benefit under a secret or half-secret trust. In *Re Rees* [1950] it was held that this was not possible but in *Re Tyler's Fund Trusts* [1967] it was suggested that such evidence is admissible.
- The death of the secret trustee before the death of the testator causes the trust to fail as the gift to the trustee lapses. But if the trust is half-secret then the trust can be valid as the will itself indicates a trust.

FURTHER THINKING

The decision in *Re Gardner* is often felt to be wrong because at the date of the beneficiary's death the trust was not constituted – this can only happen on the *testator's* death.

Are secret and half-secret trusts express or constructive?

This point is important if the trust concerns land, as in an exam question. The rule is probably that a secret trust is constructive as it is imposed to prevent fraud. A half-secret trust is probably express as it is declared on the will.

This means that secret trusts of land need not be in writing as constructive trusts of land need not be (s.53(2), LPA 1925), but half-secret trusts as express trusts are governed by s.53(1)(b), LPA 1925 which requires trusts of land other than resulting and constructive trusts to be evidenced by writing.

REVISION NOTE

Go back to Chapter 5 and check that you are clear on the formalities rules.

Chapter summary: **Putting it all together**

TEST YOURSELF

- ☐ Can you tick all the points from the **revision checklist** at the beginning of this chapter?
- ☐ Take the **end-of-chapter quiz** on the companion website.
- ☐ Test your knowledge of the cases with the **revision flashcards** on the website.
- ☐ Attempt the **essay question** from the beginning of this chapter using the guidelines below.
- ☐ Go to the companion website to try out **other questions**.

Answer guidelines

See the problem question at the start of the chapter.

A diagram illustrating how to structure your answer is available on the website.

Problem questions in this area usually contain a number of different issues and so there is plenty of opportunity to gain a really good mark. However, it is essential to have a very clear and logical structure to your answer otherwise you could get your points in the wrong order with disastrous effects on your marks! Make a plan of your answer and stick to it!

Trust to Mabel

Take the words 'for the purposes of'. Do they indicate a trust or not? An average answer will say that they do, which is probably the case, and this will mean that:

- There is definitely intention to create a trust.
- This is definitely a half-secret trust.

An excellent answer will explain that the words 'on trust' are not used and so there is the possibility that:

- There is no intention, unless the conversation in the opening paragraph indicates sufficient intention.
- Even if there is intention, which is probably the case, the trust may be secret.

If there is some doubt, then proceed for both types:

- On the basis that the trust is half-secret, there is intention, as indicated in the will but communication is doubtful. The will states that the gift to Mabel is to be 'used for the purposes which we have discussed' which indicates a past communication. In fact, communication to Mabel is by an envelope which is not to be opened until Jennifer's death and the envelope is given to Mabel on the same day as the will was executed but later on.

- Under Rule one (page 98) communication appears to be too late but, as we saw above, *Re Keen* also established that communication could be a sealed envelope not to be opened until the testator's death provided that the testator knows that the envelope contains the details of the trust. Here the words 'important instructions' could be taken as indicating that the envelope does contain details of a trust but it is not definite. The fact that communication is later in the day can probably be overlooked but the point is not decided.
- Under Rule two (page 99) communication is probably invalid as the will says 'the purposes which we have discussed' unless the initial discussion in the first paragraph can be taken as communication, which must be doubtful.
- There is probably valid communication on the basis of *Re Keen* but an excellent answer would also point out that if Rule two applies then communication is not valid as the time of communication conflicts with the will. However, there is also the long telephone conversation between Jennifer and Mabel: an excellent answer would point out that this may have contained communication.
- On the basis that the trust is secret there is valid communication as the handing over of the envelope amounts to communication before the death of the testator.
- If there is no valid communication, then Mabel will take on a resulting trust for the estate (the residuary beneficiary – the hospital). If it is valid then on we go.
- Is there a valid acceptance? There is no express acceptance but it can be implied (*Moss* v. *Cooper* (1861)) and after the initial conversation the long telephone conversation might have contained an acceptance.
- As the trust concerns land, if it is half-secret then it is express and under s.53(1)(b), LPA 1925 the trust of 'The Laurels' must be in writing. The bare details are in the will, which is of course written and, if this is sufficient, then the requirements are satisfied. An excellent answer would point out that a failure to comply with s.53(1)(b) renders the trust unenforceable and not void.
- If the trust is valid, the death of Jack will not cause the trust to fail and the gift to him will go to his estate (*Re Gardner*). (A good answer might point out that this case is considered doubtful.)

Trust to Fanny

This is secret: communication is before Jennifer's death, intention appears from the will (use of word 'trust' and acceptance can be implied).

Two problems arise:

1 Does the gift to employees, etc. satisfy the test of certainty of objects (*McPhail* v. *Doulton* [1971] – see Chapter 3)? If not, a resulting trust for the estate – in this case the hospital.

2 Can Fanny adduce evidence that she was intended to be a beneficiary? Consider *Re Rees* and *Re Tyler's Fund Trusts*.

Make your answer stand out

Pay very close attention to the actual words used in the trust. See the discussion above on whether there is any possibility that the trust to Mabel could be a secret trust.

FURTHER READING

Critchley, P. (1999) 'Instruments of Fraud: Testamentary Dispositions and Secret Trusts', 115 LQR 631. A useful look at the whole area.

Meager, R. 'Secret trusts: Do they have a Future?', 87 Conv. 203. Interesting research showing that secret trusts are important in practice.

Perrins, B. (1972) 'Can You Keep Half a Secret?', 88 LQR 225. Demonstrates that the principles in *Re Stead* rest on a tenuous historical basis.

8 Resulting trusts

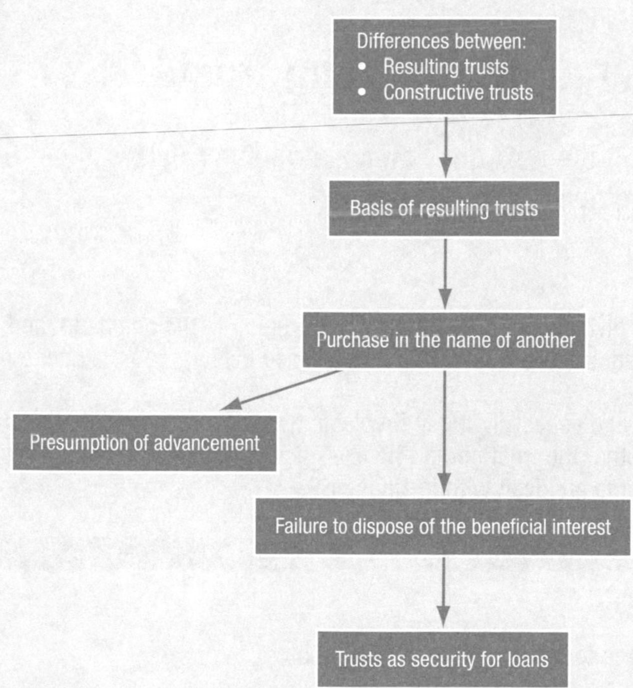

A printable version of this topic map is available from www.pearsoned.co.uk/lawexpress

Revision Checklist

Essential points you should know:

- [ ] the distinction between express trusts and resulting/constructive trusts
- [ ] the theories that explain the basis of resulting trusts
- [ ] when a resulting trust arises where property is put into the name of another and why this is so
- [ ] when a presumption of advancement arises and the significance of these today
- [ ] when a resulting trust can arise where the beneficial interest is not disposed of
- [ ] the importance of the *Quistclose* case.

Introduction:
Understanding resulting trusts

This chapter and the next one, on constructive trusts, should be considered together.

This is because:

- There is a clear dividing line between express trusts, on the one hand, and resulting and constructive trusts on the other (see below). You may get a question on this point.
- In some cases, and especially those involving trusts of the home, there can be uncertainty whether the trust should be classified as resulting or constructive. Trusts of the home are dealt with in Chapter 9.

Assessment advice

Essay questions

This is a likely area for essays which could be on:

- The basis of resulting trusts. This area is dealt with below and you should ensure that you understand the various theories, making sure that you can explain the basic idea behind them. You should then move on to relating the theories to the cases.

Assessment advice

- The basis of *Quistclose* trusts.
- Both resulting and constructive trusts looking at their common features and how they differ.

Problem questions

A problem question could link with material on constructive trusts, an obvious area being trusts of the home, or deal with *Quistclose* trusts.

Sample question

Could you answer this question? Below is a typical essay question that could arise on this topic. Guidelines on answering the question are included at the end of the chapter, whilst a sample problem question and guidance on tackling it can be found on the companion website.

Essay question

'Resulting trusts are a rag-bag of different situations with no clear principle to explain them.'

Do you agree?

Differences between express trusts and resulting and constructive trusts

The common feature of both resulting and constructive trusts is that, unlike express trusts, they are not created by the express agreement of the parties as evidenced in a trust deed, or some other writing, or, except in the case of trusts of land or an interest in land (s.53(1)(b), LPA 1925), orally. One possible exception is a secret trust (see Chapter 7) which is generally considered to be constructive but does arise from agreement.

REVISION NOTE

Go back to Chapter 7 and make sure that you are clear about what a secret trust is.

Moffat (2005: 581–582) sets out these distinctions between express trusts on the one hand, and resulting and constructive trusts on the other:

- **Functional**. Express trusts are often employed as a planning device but imputed trusts are ways of resolving disputes over ownership or entitlement to property.
- **Formal**. Express trusts must comply with certain formalities such as s.53(1)(c), LPA 1925. Imputed trusts are not affected by these (s.53(2), LPA 1925).
- **Substantive**. Express trusts arise because of some expression of intention by a property owner but imputed trusts arise by operation of some legal rule. As Moffat points out, this particular distinction breaks down in cases of disputes over the family home where intention plays a significant role.

REVISION NOTE

Go back to Chapter 5 and check that you know and understand what s.53(1)(b), s.53(1)(c) and s.53(2), LPA 1925 say.

EXAM TIP

The above points could form an excellent framework for an answer to an exam question that asks you to discuss the differences between express trusts on the one hand, and resulting and constructive trusts on the other.

Resulting trusts

Basis of resulting trusts

KEY DEFINITION

In a **resulting trust** the beneficial interest results to, or jumps back to, the settlor who created the trust. The basis of an action founded on a resulting trust is therefore that one is seeking to recover one's own property.

The idea behind resulting trusts is strange: a person (X) gives property to another (Y) and then Y ends up holding it on trust for X.

Theories to explain the basis of resulting trusts

1 Megarry J in *Re Vandervell's Trusts (No. 2)* [1974]: two types of resulting trust:

Automatic	Presumed
Nothing to do with the intentions of the settlor (e.g. where no certainty of objects) – see Chapter 3.	Where property transferred to another for no consideration (i.e. nothing given or promised in return) but no words of gift used. Megarry J felt that these did arise from the presumed intention of the settlor. This chapter contains examples of these.

Chambers (1997) points out, however, that resulting trusts are concerned with the intention of the settlor as one reason why they arise is that the settlor does not intend the property to go to the trustee (1997: 47). There is a more fundamental objection pointed out by Swadling (2008): nothing is automatic in the law. The trust does not arise automatically but because the courts say that it does.

2 Lord Browne-Wilkinson in *Westdeutsche Landesbank Girozentrale* v. *Islington BC* [1996]: resulting trusts arise from the common intention of the parties.

Example one

Joan transfers £100 to Penny to hold on trust but fails to specify the trusts. The £100 is held on trust by Penny for Joan.

FURTHER THINKING

Swadling (2008) points out that intention only arises in a negative sense as the initial intention, in the above example, was for Penny to hold the £100 on trust and so there is only a presumed intention of a resulting trust as the first intention could not be carried out. In addition can we just assume that this was the intention?

In *Re Vinogradoff* [1935] the testatrix had transferred an £800 War Loan which was in her own name into the joint names of herself and her four-year-old daughter. After the testatrix died it was held that even though the daughter had not been appointed a trustee she still held it on a resulting trust for the testatrix's estate. The fundamental point is that the court did not say that it came to this decision because of the testatrix's intentions.

3 Chambers (1997): all resulting trusts should be considered as arising from the presumption of **the lack of any intention** by the transferor to pass any beneficial interest to the transferee when the transferee has not provided the entire consideration for the property. Thus in the example above the resulting trust operates because Joan did not intend to benefit Penny.

4 Swadling (2008): Chambers' view is wrong. His argument is that the word 'presumption' needs clarification. He argues that a true presumption arises where proof of one fact generates proof of another fact without the need for further evidence. In the case of resulting trusts where the transferor puts property into the name of another the evidence is that equity originally rested the presumption on evidence that the transferor declared a trust in his own favour. 'Automatic' resulting trusts, according to Swadling, seem to have no clear foundation.

Problem area: What happens to the beneficial interest?

It is usually considered that on any transfer only the legal interest passes to the transferee and where the resulting trust arises from that transfer then a new equitable interest then arises and this is held for the transferor (see Chambers (above)). Look at the *Quistclose* case (below) to test this idea.

Cases where a resulting trust can arise

Purchase in the name of another

The basic equitable rule is that where property is purchased in the name of another then there is a presumption that the other person holds it on a resulting trust for the purchaser.

Example two

X buys a house and puts it in Y's name. There is a presumption that Y holds it on trust for X. This can be rebutted by proof that a gift was intended. (See *Dyer* v. *Dyer* (1788).)

Hodgson v. *Marks* (1971) is a good example of this point where the owner transferred her house into the name of her lodger and it was held that there was a resulting trust in her favour. Note the remarks of Russell LJ on the relationship between undue influence and resulting trusts.

Trusts of the home may come into this category. See the views of Lord Neuberger in *Abbott* v. *Abbott* (2007) and contrast them with those of Lady Hale in the same case. (See Chapter 9 for an account of the case.)

Presumption of advancement

The idea is that, in contrast to the example above where there is a presumption of a resulting trust, here there is a presumption that the person making the transfer intends an outright gift (an advancement).

The situations where a presumption can arise were rather old fashioned (e.g. they applied where a husband transfers property to his wife but not vice versa and to advancements by a father (but not a mother) to their children). However, in *Pecore* v. *Pecore* (2007) the Canadian Supreme Court held that they could also apply to an advancement by a mother. The cases also held that the presumption ceases when the child becomes an independent adult.

Read Andrews (2007) on the possiblility that the presumption contravenes Art. 5 , Protocol 7 of the European Convention on Human Rights (equality of rights and responsibilities of spouses). The extra dimension which this kind of thinking brings to an answer can really boost your marks.

An interesting area is where the presumption of a resulting trust appears to collide with the maxim that equity does not assist a person with unclean hands.

KEY CASE

***Tinsley* v. *Milligan* [1994] 1 AC 340 (HL)**

Concerning: transfers of property for unlawful purposes

Facts

A house was bought with money provided by two women (X and Y) but was only put into the name of X so that Y could (fraudulently) claim housing benefit. Y claimed that the property was held for her on a resulting trust by virtue of her contributions.

Legal principle

The issue was the conduct which Y had to rely on to support her claim of a resulting trust. If it was her fraud then she could not claim a resulting trust, in view of the principle stated above. However, here she only had to rely on her contributions to the purchase price and so her claim succeeded as her fraud was, as a matter of evidence, irrelevant.

FURTHER THINKING

This decision of the House of Lords has been strongly criticised. Look, for example, at Buckley (1994) but also note a contrary view expressed by Enonchong (1995). You should also look at the judgments of the Court of Appeal, which differed from those of the majority of the House of Lords: see *Tinsley* v. *Milligan* [1992] Ch 310 CA.

FURTHER THINKING

Consultation Paper 154 published by the Law Commission in 1999: *Illegal Transactions: The Effect of Illegality on Contracts and Trusts*, recommends that the courts should be given discretion in these cases but also sets five criteria at paragraph 1.19. Look at these carefully!

Note also *Tinker* v. *Tinker* [1970].

Failure to dispose of the beneficial interest

Example three

Re Osaba (1979): a trust was set up to maintain two women and to educate a third. After the death of the first two and the completion of the education of the third the surplus went absolutely to the third. Yet in *Re Abbott* (1982) a fund to maintain two ladies which had a surplus went to the subscribers to it. Note also *Re Gillingham Bus Disaster Fund* [1958] in Chapter 10.

REVISION NOTE

Look at Chapter 10 where this issue is looked at in connection with failure of charitable trusts. Compare the rules when a charitable fund fails with when a non-charitable one fails.

Trusts as security for loans

KEY CASE

***Barclays Bank Ltd* v. *Quistclose Investments Ltd* [1970] AC 567 (HL)**

Concerning: when a loan can be held on a resulting trust for the lender

The facts of this case do not aid an understanding of the legal principle.

Legal principle

Where a loan is made for a specific purpose which fails then a resulting trust may arise for the lender. The effect is to give the lender priority over the borrower's creditors if, as here, the borrower goes into liquidation.

KEY CASE

***Re Farepak Food and Gifts Ltd (in administration)* (2006) EWHC 3272 (HC)**

Concerning: possible application of the *Quistclose* principle

Facts

Under a Christmas hamper scheme operated by Farepak, throughout 2006 customers placed orders for hampers with Farepak's agents who then passed them on to Farepak. On 11 October 2006 Farepak decided to cease trading. Before it went into administration the directors attempted to 'ring fence' money which was received by Farepak so that it could be returned to customers. They did this by a declaration of trust and the issue was whether this had the desired effect of creating a trust.

Legal principle

The *Quistclose* principle could not apply because the money had been received by the Farepak agents (not the customers) and when it was received there was no suggestion that it was to be kept separate from other money. Thus there could be no *Quistclose* trust as there was, in effect, no trust property. There could only have been such a trust had the money from customers been kept in a separate fund so that it could not be touched until the customers had received their hampers.

FURTHER THINKING

The principle in the *Quistclose* case is controversial. Why should the lender in *Quistclose* have priority? It may be mere chance that the loan is not spent as intended. If it is spent the lender loses priority. Look at other cases on the *Quistclose* principle (e.g. *Carreras Rothmans Ltd* v. *Freeman Matthews Treasure Ltd* (1985) and Millett (1998). Another issue is who are the beneficiaries? Was it the shareholders in the *Quistclose* case?

REVISION NOTE

Check the beneficiary principle in Chapter 4.

The *Re Farepak* case is also relevant to express trusts (Chapter 3) and constructive trusts (Chapter 9). It could form an excellent illustration, in an essay question, of the modern application of the law of trusts.

Chapter summary: **Putting it all together**

TEST YOURSEFL

- [ ] Can you tick all the points from the **revision checklist** at the beginning of this chapter?
- [ ] Take the **end-of-chapter quiz** on the companion website.
- [ ] Test your knowledge of the cases with the **revision flashcards** on the website.
- [ ] Attempt the **essay question** from the beginning of this chapter using the guidelines below.
- [ ] Go to the companion website to try out **other questions**.

Answer guidelines

See the essay question at the start of the chapter.

This question requires you to know and understand the situations when a resulting trust arises and then to see if they can be linked by any coherent theory. As ever, you will not gain many marks if you just go through the situations and describe them. Instead, think about each type of trust and relate it to the theories explained at the start of this chapter. For example, you could begin with the theory of Lord Browne Wilkinson that resulting trusts can be explained on the basis of the common intention of the parties. Take a case and see if you think that this is the basis. Use the same approach for the 'automatic' theory of Megarry J in *Re Vandervell's Trusts (No. 2)* [1974] and Chambers' theory that they arise from lack of intention. Do not mention too many cases – five or six overall throughly discussed and all making different points is better than twice as many dealt with superfically.

Make your answer stand out

A really clear analysis of cases in relation to the different theories is what is required here.

FURTHER READING

Andrews, G. (2007) 'The Presumption of Advancement: Equity, Equality and Human Rights', 71 Conv. 340.

Buckley, R. (1994) 'Social Security Fraud as Illegality', 110 LQR 3.

Chambers, R. (1997) *Resulting Trusts*, Oxford: Clarendon Press.

Enonchong, N. (1995) 'Title Claims and Illegal Transactions', 111 LQR 135.

Millett, P. (1998) 'Equity's place in the Law of Commerce', 114 LQR 214.

Moffat, G. (2005) *Trusts Law: Text and Materials*, 4th edn, Cambridge: Cambridge University Press.

Swadling, W. (2008) *Explaining Resulting Trusts*, 124 LQR 72.

9 Constructive trusts

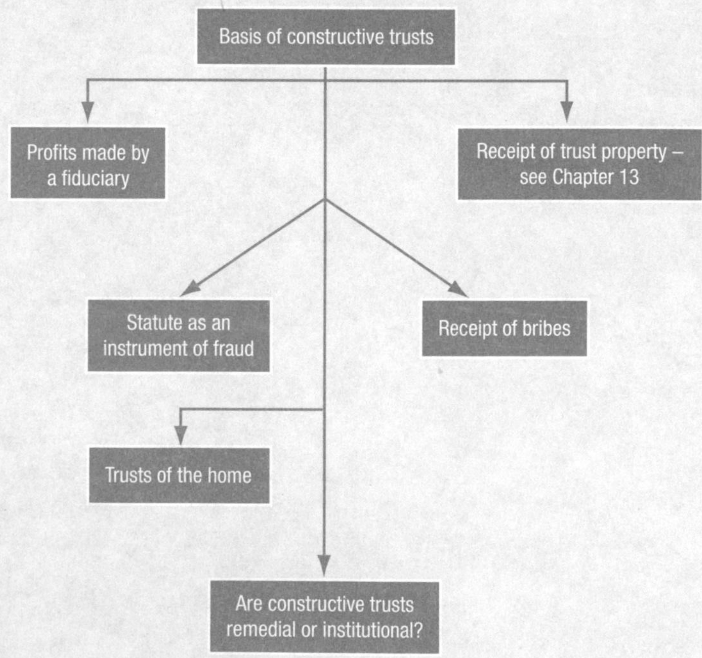

A printable version of this topic map is available from www.pearsoned.co.uk/lawexpress

Revision Checklist

Essential points you should know:

- [ ] the basis on which constructive trusts can arise
- [ ] how to identify and explain, with examples, the main situations where equity imposes a constructive trust: profits made by a fiduciary; where statute is used as an instrument of fraud; receipt of trust property by a third party
- [ ] how to identify other situations where a constructive trust has been imposed
- [ ] how to distinguish between a remedial and an institutional constructive trust.

Introduction: **Understanding constructive trusts**

It is impossible to avoid this area in an exam paper.

You may get a straight question on it, or you will find that constructive trusts come up in other areas such as trustees, breach of trust, trusts of the family home, the nature of equity and the concept of a trust. In addition the notion of a constructive trust appears in secret trusts (are these constructive?) and in the constitituon of a trust. (Where there is a *donatio mortis causa* (DMC) then this can give rise to a constructive trust.) In short, if there is one area to revise carefully, this is it! In any answer you need to be aware that there is a continuing debate about the rationale of constructive trusts. Is their development tied to the fiduciary principle or is the trust a wide-ranging remedial weapon to be used where justice demands? Read this chapter with this point in mind.

Assessment advice

Essay questions

A very familiar essay question is to ask whether there is any form of words which can explain all the circumstances when a constructive trust can arise. The answer is probably no, but you need to be able to discuss the possibilities and back up your answer with examples from the cases. This is one area where a really good knowledge of the main cases, and of any others which appeal to you, will pay dividends rather than a superficial knowledge of many cases.

Another essay scenario is to ask you to consider the difference between the institutional and the remedial constructive trust. The debates here are a bit old fashioned but still worth knowing. The case of *Binions* v. *Evans* [1972] was once an absolute staple of exam questions.

Assessment advice

Problem questions

One obvious area for a problem question is the situations where trust property has been parted with in breach of trust and where there may also be someone who has assisted in the breach. A possibility is to include with this a situation based on a *Boardman* v. *Phipps* scenario.

Sample question

Could you answer this question? Below is a typical problem question that could arise on this topic. Guidelines on answering the question are included at the end of the chapter, whilst a sample essay question and guidance on tackling it can be found on the companion website.

Problem question

Osbert is a trustee of a family trust. The trust owns shares in the Midland Optical Illusion Co. Ltd and, at a shareholders' meeting, Osbert meets Albert, a director. Albert suggests that the company is a good investment and so Osbert buys sufficient shares to give him a controlling interest in the company. At a subsequent meeting Osbert is appointed a paid director of the company.

The company has become increasingly profitable and so all of the shares have grown in value.

Advise the beneficiaries on any claims which they may have against Osbert?

Constructive trusts

What are they?

KEY DEFINITION

Millett (1998) defined **constructive trusts** as arising 'whenever the circumstances are such that it would be unconscionable for the owner of the legal title to assert his own beneficial interest and deny the beneficial interest of another'.

Can we go further than this?

Another quote is by Edmund Davies LJ in *Carl Zeiss Siftung* v. *Herbert Smith & Co. (a firm) (No. 2)* (1969):

'Its boundaries have been left perhaps deliberately vague so as not to restrict the court by technicalities in deciding what the justice of a particular case may demand.'

EXAM TIP

Essays often ask you if there is any all-embracing principle to explain when **constructive trusts** are imposed. The answer is probably no but do not forget to include in your answer trusts of the home, which are dealt with later in this next chapter.

All we can do here is indicate some circumstances when a constructive trust may be imposed:

Profits made by a fiduciary

Problem area: Defining 'fiduciary'

The concept of a 'fiduciary' and a fiduciary relationship is at the very heart of equity but attempts to define what a fiduciary is have met with difficulty. The term certainly covers relationships other then those of trustee and beneficiary and fiduciaries can include company directors and solicitors. A good place to start is Moffat (2005: 802–811).

- 'The fiduciary relationship is a concept in search of a principle' (Mason, 'Themes and prospects', in *Essays in Equity*, Finn, P. ed. (1985))
- The fiduciary concept is like 'an accordion . . . it may be expanded, or compressed, to maintain the integrity of relationships perceived to be of importance to contemporary society' (Tan, D. (1995) 69 ALJ 440).

KEY CASE

***Keech* v. *Sandford* (1726) Sel Cas Ch 61 Ct of Chan**

Concerning: persons in a fiduciary position must not use that position to make an unauthorised benefit for themselves

Facts

A trustee of a lease of a market was granted a renewal of the lease in his own name because the landlord did not wish to renew it on trust as the beneficiary was a minor who could not be bound by the usual covenants.

Legal principle

X held the renewed lease on trust for the minor even though X had neither acted fraudulently nor deprived the trust of any benefit.

KEY CASE

Boardman v. _Phipps_ [1967] 2 AC 46 (HL)

Concerning: same issue as in _Keech_ v. _Sandford_ (1726) (above) but applied in a modern context

Facts

The trust owned a substantial holding of shares in a company and the appellants were dissatisfied with its performance. They obtained information, through this connection with the trust, about the company's affairs and as a result they decided to obtain control of the company by purchasing the remainder of its shares. Having done this they reorganised it and made considerable profits for themselves. The trust could not have bought the shares without seeking the sanction of the court and it did not consider doing this.

Legal principle

The appellants were held liable to account to the trust for the profits made because they were constructive trustees as they had used the trust shareholding to acquire the necessary information about the company and in addition the respondent beneficiary had not been kept fully informed of the situation. However the appellants had acted in good faith throughout and so should be allowed 'liberal payment' for their skill in the negotiations which had resulted in the trust acquiring a considerable benefit.

KEY CASE

Queensland Mines Ltd v. _Hudson_ (1978) 18 ALR 1 (PC)

Concerning: application of the principle in _Keech_ v. _Sandford_ (1726) and _Boardman_ v. _Phipps_ [1967] to company directors

Facts

The defendant, the managing director of the claimant company, had obtained licences for the claimant to develop some mines. When the claimant found itself unable to do so the defendant, with the claimant's full knowledge, took the licences himself and developed them.

Legal principle

The defendant was not liable to account for profits made because he had not deprived the claimant of any opportunity and had kept the claimant fully informed. It is, however, difficult to reconcile this decision with *Boardman* v. *Phipps* [1967] and *Regal (Hastings) Ltd* v. *Gulliver* (1942).

Receipt of bribes

KEY CASE

***Attorney-General for Hong Kong* v. *Reid* [1994] AC 324 (HL)**

Concerning: receipt of bribes by a person in a fiduciary position

Facts

Reid, a Crown prosecutor, took bribes and then used them to buy land.

Legal principle

Where a person receive bribes in breach of their fiduciary duty then they become a constructive trustee of them and so here the bribes were the property of their employer in equity. Thus the employer was entitled to claim the profits from the bribes when they were invested.

FURTHER THINKING

Although this decision clearly has much to commend it on the level of ensuring that a person who takes bribes does not benefit by simply investing them, it also has the result that where a person has taken bribes and invested the proceeds the employer can claim these. Thus if the person is bankrupt, as here, the employer is in a better position than the unsecured creditors of that person.

Statute as an instrument of fraud

See Rochefoucauld v. *Boustead* [1897] in Chapter 5. However, the next case shows that equity does not always intervene to set aside a statutory requirement: there may be other more important values at stake.

KEY CASE

***Midland Bank Trust Co. Ltd* v. *Green* [1981] AC 513 (HL)**

Concerning: whether a statutory requirement should be set aside as it is an instrument of fraud

Facts

An option granted by a father to his son to purchase a farm had not been registered as required by the Land Charges Act 1972 and the father, having changed his mind about the sale, then carried out a 'sham' sale to his wife so that his son's option was then defeated.

KEY CASE

Legal principle

The son's claim failed, Lord Wilberforce observing that 'it is not fraud to rely on legal rights conferred by an Act of Parliament'.

Trusts of the home

This is an important area for exams and can also arise in a land law exam. The courts have used the concepts of both resulting and constructive trusts. Here is an example based on a typical exam question.

Example one

Jane and her boyfriend Tom moved into a house which was in Jane's name as she was able to get a mortgage. However, it was always intended to be their joint home and Jane said to Tom: 'This will be our joint home for life. We will settle here.' Tom agreed and said that as this was the case, he would pay the deposit. The house needed a great deal of renovation and Tom spent all of his spare time working on the house.

Two years later Jane met Algy and told Tom: 'Algy is the man in my life now. You will have to move out.'

Does Tom have any rights in the house?
Tom may have three claims:

1. Based on a resulting trust as he had contributed to the purchase of the house which was in Jane's name.
2. Based on a constructive trust based not only on his contributions to the purchase but the work which he did on the house.
3. Based on estoppel which will be similar to the constructive trust claim but emphasises detrimental reliance, i.e. he relied on Jane's statement.

REVISION NOTE

Check Chapter 8 for resulting trusts and Chapter 6 for estoppel.

How does the law deal with this situation?

This is an excellent study in the development of constructive trusts which could be used to illustrate an essay question. Your answer should mention three stages of development:

1 The approach of the Court of Appeal in the 1970s under the leadership of Denning MR based on the remedial constructive trust. *Eves* v. *Eves* [1975] is a very good (and memorable) example of this.
2 The swing back to a more orthodox approach in the 1980s. *Burns* v. *Burns* [1984] is a good instance of this and the law was restated by the House of Lords in *Lloyds Bank plc* v. *Rosset* [1991]. The judgment of Lord Bridge was, for a long time, accepted as the authority on this subject.
3 Very recent developments in the cases of *Stack* v. *Dowden* (2007) and *Abbott* v. *Abbott* (2007) which have shown a tendency to go back to the Court of Appeal's 1970s approach.

Note this quote from Lady Hale in *Abbott* v. *Abbott* (2007).

> 'a person could acquire a beneficial interest in another's land under a general enquiry as to their common intention and this could include intention which was actual, imputed from conduct or inferred provided that there was a direct or indirect contribution, in cash or in kind, to the acquisition of the land'.

Compare this with Lord Bridge's speech in *Rosset* [1991].

Tom, in the example above, would have a valid claim under any of the three approaches above but what if he had neither made any contribution nor had Jane said that the house was to be their joint home? This is what, in effect, occurred in *Burns* v. *Burns* and the issue is whether equity should provide a remedy and, if so, on what principles it should be based.

EXAM TIP

In an essay question, do not just criticise the cases. It is all too easy to say that, for example, Valerie Burns in *Burns* v. *Burns* was badly treated. What do you suggest that the law should be? It is the test of a good student not only to suggest that the law is unjust but also to suggest realistic alternatives.

This is an important area. Do make use of the further reading suggested at the end of this chapter.

FURTHER THINKING

Have a look at the Law Commission's proposals for change in this area and ask yourself how they link with the approach of Lady Hale in the House of Lords in the *Stack* v. *Dowden* and *Abbott* v. *Abbott* cases: 'Cohabitation: The Financial Consequences of Relationship Breakdown' (Law Com. Report 307).

FURTHER THINKING

Are constructive trusts institutional or remedial?

In a series of cases in the 1970s Denning MR sought to develop what he called 'a constructive trust of a new model' *(Eves* v. *Eves* (1975)). The existence of a fiduciary relationship was not required to found such a trust: instead one would be imposed 'whenever justice and good conscience require it . . . it is an equitable remedy by which the court can enable an aggrieved party to obtain restitution' (Denning MR in *Hussey* v. *Palmer* (1972)). The main areas in which the new model constructive trust has been used are in disputes over the home (see above) and the enforceability of contractual licences as in *Binions* v. *Evans* [1972].

There are two objections to the new model constructive trust:

1 To look at a constructive trust as a remedy and not as a substantive institution is wrong because, even though constructive trusts have always been remedies in one sense (see the cases above), they have also been substantive trusts because the property is trust property and therefore if the trustee becomes bankrupt the beneficiaries take priority over the trustee's creditors.

2 The idea of imposing a constructive trust whenever justice requires leads to uncertainty. Mahon J memorably observed in the New Zealand case of *Carly* v. *Farrelly* (1975): 'No stable system of jurisprudence can permit a litigant's claim to justice to be consigned to the formless void of individual moral opinion.'

The new model constructive trust was firmly rejected by the Court of Appeal in *Halifax Building Society* v. *Thomas* (1995) and *Re Polly Peck International plc (No. 2)* (1998) and you should also note *Re Farepak Food and Gifts Limited (in administation)* (2006) (Chapter 8) and *Farah Constructions Pty Ltd and others* v. *Say-Dee Pty Ltd* (2007) (Chapter 13).

This debate is fundamentally about whether a constructive trust should be tied to equitable principles, albeit functioning as a remedy in one sense as in *Boardman* v. *Phipps* [1967] or if it should simply be a general remedy, taking its place alongside damages and injunctions (see Gardner 2003: 121–127).

Chapter summary: **Putting it all together**

TEST YOURSELF

- ☐ Can you tick all the points from the **revision checklist** at the beginning of this chapter?
- ☐ Take the **end-of-chapter quiz** on the companion website.
- ☐ Test your knowledge of the cases with the **revision flashcards** on the website.
- ☐ Attempt the **essay question** from the beginning of this chapter using the guidelines below.
- ☐ Go to the companion website to try out **other questions**.

Answer guidelines

See the essay question at the start of the chapter.

- Trustees are in a fiduciary position: explanation of the term 'fiduciary' – Osbert has taken advantage of his position to purchase shares and obtain an appointment as fee paying director.
- Apply case law: *Keech* v. *Sandford*, and especially *Boardman* v. *Phipps*. Need to contrast these with *Queensland Mines Ltd* v. *Hudson*.
- It is almost certain that Osbert will hold on constructive trust.
- Will the court allow 'liberal payment' as in *Boardman*? Probably not as here Osbert's conduct is a clearer breach than that of *Boardman*.

Make your answer stand out

A thorough knowledge of *Boardman* v. *Phipps* and an ability to see the contrast with *Queensland Mines Ltd* v. *Hudson* is essential. Research detail on other cases.

FURTHER READING

Dixon, M. (2005) 'Resulting and Constructive Trusts of Land; the Mist Descends and Rises', 69 Conv. 79.

Dixon, M. (2007) 'The never-ending story – co-ownership after *Stack* v. *Dowden*', Conv. 456.

Gardner, S. (1993) 'Rethinking Family Property', 109 LQR 263.

Gardner, S. (2003) *An Introduction to the Law of Trusts*, 2nd edn, Oxford: Oxford University Press.

Millett, P. (1998) 'Restitution and Constructive Trusts', 114 LQR 399.

Moffatt, G. (2005) *Trusts Law: Text and Materials*, 4th edn, Cambridge: Cambridge University Press.

Rotherham, C. (2004) 'The Property Rights of Unmarried Cohabitees: a Case for Reform', 68 Conv. 268. An excellent general survey.

Swadling, W. (2007) 'The Common Intention Constructive Trust in the House of Lords: an Opportunity Missed, LQR 511.

10 Charitable trusts

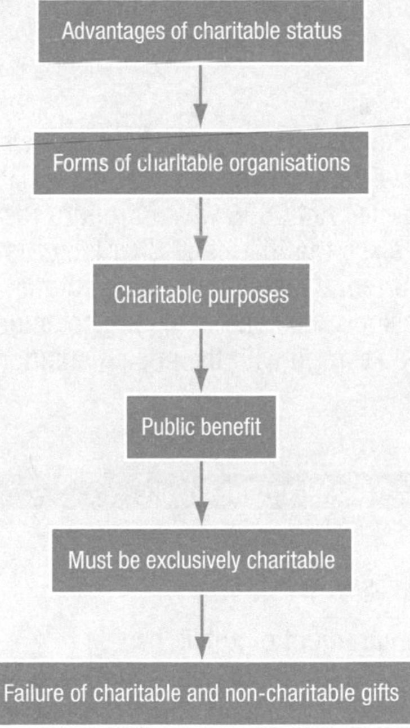

A printable version of this topic map is available from www.pearsoned.co.uk/lawexpress

Revision Checklist

Essential points you should know:

- [ ] what is meant by charitable purposes
- [ ] what is meant by public benefit and what this means in the context of each head of charity
- [ ] charitable trusts must be exclusively charitable
- [ ] the scope of the *cy-près* doctrine and the position when it does not apply.

Introduction:
Understanding charitable trusts

This is one of the most common areas for questions in an equity exam paper.

It lends itself to both essay and problem questions neither of which are too difficult but they do require a good knowledge of case law. It is essential that you are aware of the main provisions of the Charities Act 2006 which brought the first major change in the statute law on this subject since the Statute of Charitable Uses Act 1601. You also need to be up to date on the current debate on what constitutes public benefit. The website of the Charity Commission (www.charity-commission.gov.uk) is an excellent place to start your research. Do keep up with the implementation timetable of the Act – also available on this website.

Assessment advice

Essay questions

There are two main possible essay questions:

1. Essay questions on the requirement of public benefit.
2. A more general essay question on the Charities Act 2006, possibly looking at the place of charities in society in the light of the changes made by the Act. You do need to look at the background to the Act and be able to discuss the main controversial issues (e.g. the extent to which public benefit should be required for a charitable trust).

▶

Assessment advice

Problem questions

There are two main possible problem questions:

1 Problem questions on whether particular objects of a trust are charitable.
2 Problem questions on the failure of charitable gifts.

The first area is the most likely and it will require you to know and be able to apply the relevant part of the Charities Act and also to discuss the extent to which cases decided under the previous law are still relevant. Select some cases and test them against the new law.

Note very precisely what the question asks you to do. It may either ask you to advise on whether the gift (often in a will) is charitable or to advise on the validity of the gift. If it is the latter then, if you decide that the gift cannot be charitable, you need to ask if it could be valid as a private trust or, possibly, if it comes under one of the cases where non-charitable trusts are valid.

Sample question

Could you answer this question? Below is a typical problem question that could arise on this topic. Guidelines on answering the question are included at the end of the chapter, whilst a sample essay question and guidance on tackling it can be found on the companion website.

Problem question

Albert, by will, left the following bequests:

(a) £10,000 to the Worcester Women's Benevolent Society which provides grants to elderly women in Worcester who are in need.
(b) £15,000 to the Faith Society which welcomes those of any faith or none to join them in their quest for spiritual enlightenment.
(c) £20,000 to provide scholarships to enable children resident in Worcester to attend university, preference to be given to children of workers employed in the porcelain industry in Worcester.
(d) The residue of his property on trust to be used for such charitable, humanitarian or benevolent causes as his trustees may select.

Can you advise Albert's trustees on the validity of these gifts?

Advantages of charitable status

This topic can appear in an essay question and you should be prepared to discuss it under two heads:

1 legal
2 fiscal, i.e. taxation.

You are unlikely to be asked a detailed question on the fiscal advantages and so concentrate on the legal ones:

(a) Trusts for non-charitable purposes are generally void (see Chapter 4) as there is no one to enforce them, but the Attorney-General can enforce charitable trusts and, in practice, the Charity Commissioners police the charity sector. There is scope here for a good answer which thinks laterally by linking material on both types of purpose trusts – charitable and non-charitable – and compares them from the point of view of enforceability.
(b) The requirement of certainty of objects does not apply to charitable trusts. Once again impress the examiner with lateral thinking and draw a comparison with private trusts.

REVISION NOTE

See, for example, *McPhail* v. *Doulton* [1971] in Chapter 3.

(c) The rule against perpetuities applies to charities (see Chapter 4) but, and this is the vital point, a gift over from one charity to another is not subject to the rules.

Rule against perpetuity

EXAM TIP

Taking point (c) above, it is worth taking time to be absolutely clear about what this means as very few students do so and it will be a real plus point for you in the exam!

REVISION NOTE

The Rule also appears in Chapter 4 in another context and so knowledge of it will be useful in two possible exam questions.

The idea in this context is that a gift should not vest at too remote a time in the future and if it does so then it is void.

Too remote a future time is defined as beyond lives or lives in being plus 21 years, but the point as far as charities are concerned is that a gift over from one charity to another which takes place beyond this is not affected by the rule. The effect is that you demonstrate knowledge of the rule and then show that it does not apply to charities.

Example one

Jack by will leaves all his estate to Hanbury School, a registered charity, but provides that if the school shall ever cease to exist then any remaining funds from the estate not used shall go to the Hospital of St John. Clearly this may take place long after anyone now alive is dead and indeed beyond 21 years from their death too. Even so, the gift is valid.

EXAM TIP

Take some time to master the above point. Greater detail will not be needed: just clarity about the precise point!

Forms of charitable organisations

This is really just background detail but it will stop you making fundamental errors! Although charity law is a part of the law of trusts (because charities were enforced by equity and not the common law) a charity can exist as:

- a trust
- a company
- an unincorporated association, i.e. a body which is not a company and which has technically no legal existence – see Chapter 4 for more on this.

Definition of charity

Three basic tests for charitable status exist (see Figure 10.1).

EXAM TIP

Make sure that in a problem question you apply each of these tests to each situation.

Figure 10.1

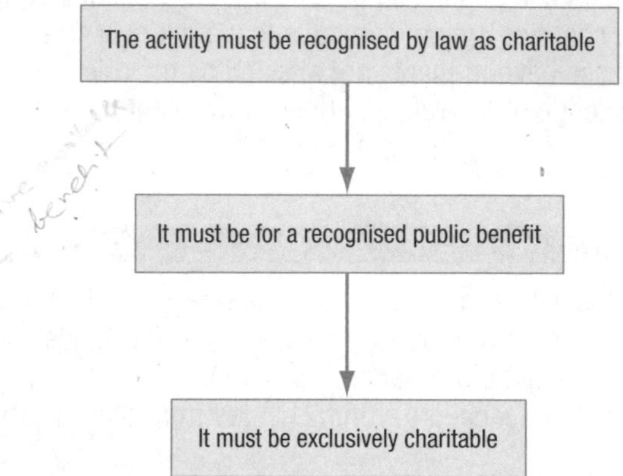

Charitable purposes recognised by law

Section 2 of the Charities Act 2006 sets out the charitable purposes recognised by law. This Act fundamentally overhauled charity law.

(a) Prevention or relief of poverty

KEY CASE

***Re Coulthurst* [1951] Ch 661 (HC)**

Concerning: meaning of 'poverty' in charity law

The facts of this case do not aid an understanding of the legal principle.

Legal principle

Evershed MR said that 'poverty does not mean destitution . . . it may not be unfairly paraphrased as meaning persons who have to "go short"'.

KEY CASE

***Re Niyazi's Will Trusts* [1978] 3 All ER 785 (HC)**

Concerning: application of the meaning of poverty in charity law

Facts

A gift was left as a contribution to the cost of building a 'working men's hostel'.

Legal principle

This was charitable, even though there was no express limitation to those who were poor as the words 'working men' and 'hostel' indicated those with a lower income.

(b) Advancement of education

Exam questions often deal with trusts for research: are they educational?

KEY CASE

***Re Hopkins' Will Trusts* [1965] Ch 669 (HC)**

Concerning: meaning of education

Facts

A trust for the promotion of research into finding the Bacon–Shakespeare manuscripts was held charitable.

Legal principle

Education must be used in a wide sense and extends beyond teaching. Research must either

- be of educational value to the researcher, or
- pass into the store of educational material or improve the sum of communicable knowledge.

(c) Advancement of religion

KEY CASE

***Thornton* v. *Howe* (1862) 31 Beav 14 Ct of Chan**

Concerning: trusts for the advancement of religion

Facts

A trust to promote the writings of Joanna Southcote, who founded a small sect and who proclaimed that she was with child by the Holy Ghost and would give birth to a second Messiah, was held charitable.

Legal principle

Provided that the trust exists for the advancement of religion the court will not say that it fails as a charity because it disapproves of its beliefs. However, note the comments of Goff J in *Church of Scientology* v. *Kaufman* (1973) below.

FURTHER THINKING

The Charities Act contains an extended definition of religion to include non-deity and multi-deity groups. To what extent will this change the law, if at all? Read *Hansard*, 3 February and 10 February 1988, which are debates on the decision to refuse registration as a charity to the Unification Church (The Moonies). Harding (2008) has an excellent discussion in the light of the requirements of the Charities Act 2006.

EXAM TIP

This is a good point to note that the courts do make judgments, assisted by expert evidence, on the value of the trust in, for example, educational or religious terms. An example is Goff J in *Church of Scientology* v. *Kaufman* (1973) who described the objects of the church as 'pernicious nonsense'.

Heads of charity

The new heads under the Charities Act 2006 are as follows. The following list begins at (d) as (a) poverty, (b) education and (c) religion have been discussed above:

(d) Advancement of health or the saving of lives.
(e) Advancement of citizenship or community development.
(f) Advancement of the arts, culture, heritage or science.

(g) Advancement of amateur sport. (Note that sport only qualifies if it involves physical exertion.)
(h) Advancement of human rights, conflict resolution or reconciliation or the promotion of religious or racial harmony or equality and diversity. (See below under the discussion of political trusts.)
(i) Advancement of environmental protection or improvement.
(j) Relief of those in need by reason of youth, old age, ill health, disability, financial hardship or other disadvantage.
(k) Advancement of animal welfare.
(l) The promotion of the efficiency of the armed forces of the Crown.
(m) Other purposes currently recognised as charitable and any new charitable purposes which are similar to another charitable purpose.

EXAM TIP

In an exam question on the changes in the definition of charity in the Charities Act 2006 you should point out four things:

1 Many of these objects simply make a particular object specifically charitable when before it was included under the general fourth head (e.g. animal welfare).
2 In some cases the object formed part of an existing object and is now on its own: for example, advancement of the arts, heritage or science would previously have come mainly under education.
3 In some cases the new charitable objects may go further than the existing ones (e.g. promotion of amateur sport).
4 In other cases the law is brought into line with the current practice of the Charity Commission (e.g. new definition of religion, etc.).

EXAM TIP

Make sure that in a problem question you apply each of these tests to each situation.

When revising do not just memorise the new heads of charity but instead do two things:

1 Look at each head in the light of the above bullet points.
2 Do some deeper research into perhaps four of them: there will not be time in an exam question to say something useful about them all.

The Charities Act also preserves some other existing charitable purposes, for example, under the Recreational Charities Act 1958, which makes recreational *facilities* charitable.

EXAM TIP

If you see a mention of, for example, village halls and sports centres in a question then it is likely that the Recreational Charities Act 1958 will be relevant.

Requirement of a recognised public benefit

In order to be charitable the objects of a trust must be for the benefit of a section of the public. A trust set up for the education of named children, for example, would not be charitable (*Re Compton* (1945)).

This is where the Charities Act 2006 makes a major change and you must be aware of it for the exam: Under the previous law:

- The advancement of education and religion were presumed in principle to benefit the public although actual benefit still needed to be proved.
- There was hardly any requirement that trusts for the relief of poverty had to be for the public benefit.
- Public benefit had to be proved in charities under the fourth head. (This was a general head defined as other purposes beneficial to the community.)

Under the Charities Act 2006:

- Public benefit must be proved in all cases and it is no longer assumed that education and religion are by themselves beneficial to the public. In addition trusts for the relief of poverty will in future have to prove public benefit.

EXAM TIP

Do some research on the effect which this will have. Independent schools are a good example.

Key principles

The Charity Commission has set out two key principles of public benefit which are essential to learn for exams:

1 There must be an identifiable benefit(s).
   1a: It must be clear what the benefits are
   1b: The benefits must be related to the aims
   1c: Benefits must be balanced against any detriment or harm.

2 Benefit must be to the public, or a section of the public.
   2a: The beneficiaries must be appropriate to the aims
   2b: Where benefit is to a section of the public, the opportunity to benefit must not be unreasonably restricted:

- by geographical or other restrictions
- by ability to pay any fees charged

2c: People in poverty must not be excluded from the opportunity to benefit
2d: Any private benefits must be incidental.

The Charity Commission website has more information on these principles and also on the supplementary guidance which it is issuing on public benefit and particular types of charity (e.g. education and religion). It is absolutely essential that you keep up to date with what is happening here.

You will find the following cases on public benefit decided under the old law still useful as existing case law will be used to decide if there is public benefit but you must relate them to the above principles.

KEY CASE

***Dingle* v. *Turner* [1972] 1 All ER 878 (HL)**

Concerning: requirement of public benefit in poverty cases

Facts

The object of the trust was to apply the income from a fund to pay pensions to poor employees and ex-employees of a company.

Legal principle

This was charitable as trusts for poor employees (and for poor relations) were charitable. The court felt that it could not overrule case law which had existed for more than 200 years.

Note: This case is included to give you material for essay questions on the impact of the Charities Act 2006 as the principle in this case has now been altered by the Act

KEY CASE

***Oppenheim* v. *Tobacco Securities Trust Co. Ltd* [1951] AC 297 (HL)**

Concerning: public benefit in trusts for the advancement of education

Facts

A trust was set up for the education of children of employees or ex-employees of British American Tobacco.

Legal principle

This was not charitable as there was a personal connection: all the beneficiaries were connected with the same company.

FURTHER THINKING

The decision in *Oppenheim* has been criticised, especially given that the company had over 100,000 employees and so the potential beneficiaries were a very large number. Read Lord McDermott's noteable dissenting judgment.

KEY CASE

Re Koettgen's Will Trusts [1954] Ch 252 (HC)

Concerning: public benefit where there was a preference for a limited class

Facts

A trust for commercial education provided that preference should be given to employees of a named company of up to 75 per cent of income.

Legal principle

This was charitable as a preference for a private group does not necessarily mean that there is no public benefit.

EXAM TIP

This case often comes up in problem questions and you should be familiar with the facts, as the problem will have slightly different ones. It is likely that a trust which provided that a greater proportion of the income would go to the preferential class (e.g. 85 per cent) would not be valid.

KEY CASE

Gilmour v. *Coates* [1949] AC 426 (HL)

Concerning: requirement of public benefit in trusts for the advancement of religion

Facts

A gift was left by a will to a convent of nuns who were strictly cloistered and who had no contact with the outside world.

Legal principle

This was not charitable as there was no evidence of public benefit. The prayers of the nuns could not be said to benefit the public as there was no proof of this.

FURTHER THINKING

The attitude of the courts to public benefit had caused controversy and it has been suggested that at times it was too strict. Read Moffat (2005: 965–975) which has an excellent critique of the law. Look also at the Reports of the Charity Commission – available on its website.

Political trusts

A trust which has objects which are political cannot be charitable. The reason is that it is not for the courts to decide if what may be a controversial purpose should be for the public benefit given the tax advantages which charities have.

KEY CASE

***McGovern* v. *Attorney-General* [1981] 3 All ER 493 (HC)**

Concerning: trusts for political objects

Facts

Amnesty International set up a trust with these objects:

(a) relief of needy persons who were, or might be, prisoners of conscience
(b) attempting to secure their release
(c) abolition of torture or other inhumane methods of treatment or punishment
(d) research into human rights.

Legal principle

Objects (a) and (d) were charitable but (b) and (c) were political as they were designed to change the policies of governments and/or change the law. Thus the trust was not charitable.

FURTHER THINKING

This case led to much discussion (e.g. see Chesterman (1999) and subsequent reports of the Charity Commissioners, in particular the most recent guidance issued by the Charity Commissioners). Research the extent to which the new head of charity (h) (human rights etc.) will enable charities to engage in activities (b) and (c) in *McGovern* (above).

Must be exclusively charitable

A gift cannot be charitable if one or more of its purposes are not charitable.

Always check for this last requirement in an exam question: it is sometimes forgotten! A good case on this point is *McGovern* v. *A-G* [1981] (above).

KEY CASE

***Chichester Diocesan Fund and Board of Finance Inc.* v. *Simpson* (1944) AC 341 (HL)**

Concerning: requirement that a trust must be exclusively charitable

Facts

A trust was established for 'charitable or benevolent objects'.

Legal principle

It was not exclusively charitable as the words 'or benevolent' implied that the trust existed for objects which were not charitable.

EXAM TIP

This case often appears in exam questions and there may be a variation to 'charitable and benevolent objects'. This will make the trust charitable as the word 'or' implies two objects, one of which (benevolent) is not charitable, but 'and' implies just one, which is charitable. However, it must be said that such nit picking does equity little credit!

EXAM TIP

In a problem question on charities watch carefully for what the question asks you to do:

- Advise whether the gifts are valid charitable gifts.
- Advise whether the gifts are valid.

In this second case you will gain extra marks by looking at whether the gift could take effect as a valid private trust or perhaps a valid non-charitable purpose trust (see Chapter 4) if it is not charitable.

Failure of charitable and non-charitable gifts

A gift to a particular body, whether a charity or not, may fail because, for example,

- the body no longer exists
- it had never existed
- it had been amalgamated with another body.

In these cases, we need to decide where the gift goes to. It could be held on a resulting trust for the donor, or their estate. However, the law is reluctant, especially where the gift was intended for charitable purposes, to allow it to go away from the charitable sector, and so it is possible for the gift to be applied for similar charitable purposes under the *cy-près* doctrine.

KEY DEFINITION

Cy-près: this means 'so near'.

EXAM TIP

This usually appears as a separate exam question and is likely to be a problem. It may involve gifts for non-charitable purposes as well, which is why they are also dealt with here. You may get what is in effect a two-part question: the first part asks you if the gift is charitable and then you are asked to deal with the position where it has failed.

Failure of charitable gifts

Example two

Richard by will leaves £10,000 to his old school, Wigorn College. However, at the date of his death, the school had ceased to exist. Advise the trustees of Richard's will.

The first question is whether the gift was for charitable purposes. The answer seems to be yes, although extra marks here for mentioning that under the Charities Act the public benefit requirement is tighter.

Assuming that it is, you need to discuss ***cy-près*** application. This will allow the gift to be applied for purposes *cy-près* (so near) (i.e. as near as possible) to the original purposes (see Figure 10.2).

Figure 10.2

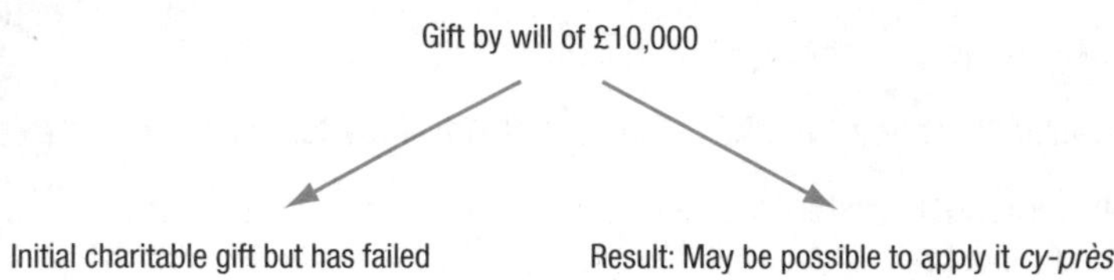

The result is that, returning to the example, two requirements must be satisfied:

1 The donor (Richard) must have shown a general charitable intention, i.e. not just to benefit that school but educational charity in a more general way (e.g. see *Re Rymer* (1895)). Note also *Re Harwood* (1936): easier to find a general charitable intention where the body had never existed at all.
2 The gift has failed within the meaning of the Charities Act 1993, s.13 (to be replaced by similar provisions in the Charities Act 2006).

Suppose that this is not so. Then there is another possibility: has the school amalgamated with another school so that that school is carrying on its purposes? If so, then it may claim the gift (see *Re Faraker* (1912).

If the problem is that there is no general charitable intention then *Re Slevin* (1891) may come to the rescue as shown in Figure 10.3.

Figure 10.3

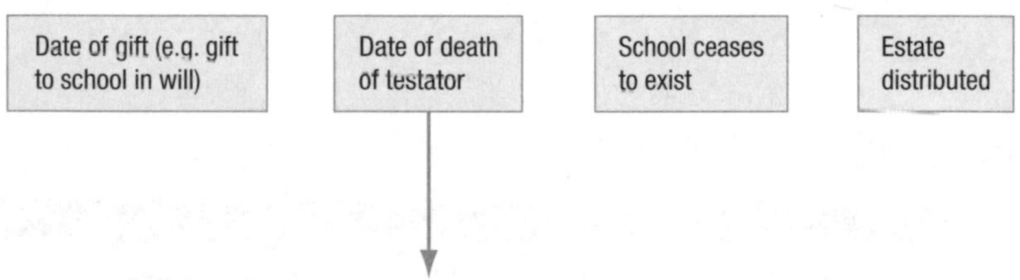

Thus, in the above example, if the school existed at the date of Richard's death but before the £10,000 was paid over, no general charitable intention need be shown for *cy-près* to apply. This is known as subsequent failure.

The above discussion has assumed that the school operates as a company, which is likely because of legal liabilities. Suppose that it was an unincorporated association?

REVISION NOTE

Remember that these do not exist in law as such and this can have unfortunate consequences which we considered in Chapter 4.

However, if the gift fails as the association ceases to exist then unincorporated association status is a positive advantage as the gift was never made to the association anyway. So, provided that its purposes are still continuing, the gift can go to a body which is carrying them on. (See *Re Finger's Will Trusts* [1972].)

Failure of non-charitable gifts

Suppose that we are not dealing with a charitable gift at all. This will be so where the purposes are not charitable and this usually arises in two situations in exams:

Situation One	Situation two
Donations are made to a disaster fund which turns out not to be charitable (e.g. see *Re Gillingham Bus Disaster Fund* [1959]). A surplus remains. In *Re Gillingham* it was held that it went on a resulting trust for the donors, even if they could not be found.	A social club is wound up. (Revision point: why isn't it charitable?) What happens to the surplus? Two possibilities: 1 It goes to the members – see e.g. *Re Bucks Constabulary Fund (No. 2)* (1979) 2 It goes to the Crown as *bona vacantia* – see *Re West Sussex Constabulary Fund* [1970].

Section 14 of the Charities Act 2006 allows a charity appeal to state that if the charitable purposes fail, gifts will be applied *cy-près*.

FURTHER THINKING

This area is unsatisfactory and you should consider the alternative possibilities. For a really good mark, read Chambers (1997: 61–67).

Chapter summary: Putting it all together

TEST YOURSELF

- [ ] Can you tick all the points from the **revision checklist** at the beginning of this chapter?
- [ ] Take the **end-of-chapter quiz** on the companion website.
- [ ] Test your knowledge of the cases with the **revision flashcards** on the website.
- [ ] Attempt the **essay question** from the beginning of this chapter using the guidelines below.
- [ ] Go to the companion website to try out **other questions**.

Answer guidelines

See the problem question at the start of the chapter.

In each case, ask three questions:

1 Is the gift for charitable purposes?
2 If so, is there sufficient public benefit?
3 If so, is it exclusively charitable?

Remember: unless it is absolutely certain that the gift does not satisfy 1 you should go on to consider 2, and the same applies to 2 and 3.

(a) Gift may be for the relief of poverty but is there a public benefit?
(b) Is the society for the advancement of religion? If not, could it come under other heads?
(c) The purpose is educational but a public benefit? Look at *Oppenheim* and *Re Koettgen*.
(d) Exclusively charitable? *Chichester Diocesan Fund* v. *Simpson*. Humanitarian?

Make your answer stand out

In (b) adopt an imaginative approach to where the purpose could fit in.
In (c) exhibit a clear knowledge of the facts of *Re Koettgen* and knowledge of critical approaches to the law (e.g. Lord McDermott's dissenting judgment in *Oppenheim*).

FURTHER READING

Chambers, R. (1997) *Resulting Trusts*, Oxford: Oxford University Press.

Chesterman, M. (1999) 'Foundations of Charity Law in the New Welfare State', 62 MLR 333.

Harding, M. (2008) 'Trusts for Religious Purposes and the Question of Public Benefit', 71 MLR 159.

Moffat, G. (2005) *Trusts Law and Materials*, 4th edn, Cambridge: Cambridge University Press.

11 Trusteeship

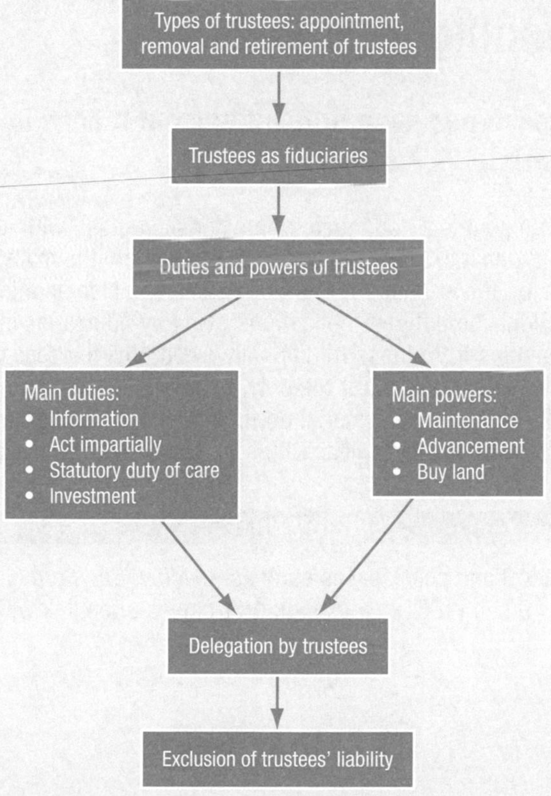

A printable version of this topic map is available from www.pearsoned.co.uk/lawexpress

Revision Checklist

Essential points you should know:

- [ ] the rules on appointment, retirement and removal of trustees (in brief)
- [ ] the meaning of the term 'fiduciary' and its implications for trustees
- [ ] the distinction between duties and powers of trustees
- [ ] the main duties and powers
- [ ] the extent to which trustees may delegate
- [ ] the extent to which the trust instrument may exclude the liability of trustees.

Introduction:
Understanding trusteeship

The topic of trusteeship is not a difficult one but it does involve a good deal of material.

It is a practical area and so it is a good idea to familiarise yourself with an actual trust instrument to see what one looks like and to be able to identify the main types of clauses. (There is one on the website for this book.) There is also an interesting shift in the case law to recognising different obligations owed by fiduciaries in some types of commercial relationships from those traditionally owed. See the cases below on exclusion of liability. Note that this is not the only chapter in which trustees are considered: Chapter 9 also contains material on the fiduciary duties of trustees and you should make sure that you are familiar with it before starting this chapter.

REVISION NOTE

Refer back to Chapter 9 and check cases such as *Keech* v. *Sandford* (1726) and *Boardman* v. *Phipps* 9 sub (1967). Questions on trustees often link with constructive trusts.

Assessment advice

Essay questions

This is a likely area for an essay question with possibilities of questions on:

- the extent of the duties of trustees, of which an example is set out below
- the fiduciary principle, where you can use your knowledge of the constructive trust cases
- the changes made by the Trustee Act 2000: this is getting a bit old hat now but examiners may still ask it
- the relationship between the statutory duties and powers of trustees and those in a trust instrument.

Problem questions

Questions are likely on the application of a range of duties and powers. For example, a common question examines powers of maintenance and advancement, or investment possibly combined with delegation. Do remember that the Trustee Act 1925 applies to maintenance and advancement but other areas are governed by the Trustee Act 2000. Again a question may bring in the scenario in *Boardman* v. *Phipps* (1967) and link it with other topics which are governed by the Trustee Act 2000 (e.g. trustees' right to remuneration). In all questions identify at the start if a duty and/or a power is involved and state clearly the different principles applicable to the relevant one.

Sample question

Could you answer this question? Below is a typical problem question that could arise on this topic. Guidelines on answering the question are included at the end of the chapter, whilst a sample essay question and guidance on tackling it can be found on the companion website.

Problem question

Arthur died in 2004. His will appointed Steve and Bryn as trustees of a fund worth £500,000 to hold for the benefit of Arthur's children Kate (aged 25), Sue (aged 21) and Mary (aged 16), contingent on them reaching the age of 30.

You are asked to advise the trustees on the following:

(a) Kate, who works in an investment bank, has told them that it would be an excellent idea to invest the bulk of the fund in a company specialising in property developments in France as 'there is certain to be a property boom there next year'. If the trustees hand over the money to Kate then she is prepared to take care of the investment details.

(b) Steve thinks that it would be a good idea to invest some of the money in a small private company run by Terry, a friend of his. Terry has offered to appoint Steve a paid director if this happens.

(c) Sue would like £70,000 of 'her money' to be paid to her now as she wishes to set up a hairdressing business. She has recently qualified as a hairdresser.

(d) Mary would like the sum of £500 paid to her each year so that she can receive singing lessons in Milan.

Appointment of trustees

EXAM TIP

It is unlikely that an exam question will ask you to deal with this area in detail. However, you may get a question on the relationship between the powers contained in the trust instrument and statutory powers so this area gives you a useful illustration.

Appointment of trustees is normally made in the first instance by the settlor or testator in the instrument or will which creates the trust. What happens later when existing trustees need to be replaced? This is where the statutory power in s.36(1) of the Trustee Act 1925 (TA 1925) comes in, as it lists eight cases where trustees who, for example, die, wish to be discharged, etc. can be replaced by the remaining trustees. In addition, appointment also brings in the other element, that of control by the court as under s.41, TA 1925 the court can appoint new trustees where it is 'impracticable or inexpedient to do so without the assistance of the court'.

Retirement and removal of trustees

This also involves the relationship between the statutory powers and the trust instrument although in the case of removal it is more likely that this will be done by the court. Retirement of trustees is governed by s.39, TA 1925 and removal is governed by the general powers of the court.

Trustees as fiduciaries

REVISION NOTE

Go back to Chapter 9 and check that you are clear what a fiduciary is.

An excellent quote on trustees as fiduciaries is as follows:

> '[A trustee] is not, unless expressly provided, entitled to make a profit; he is not allowed to put himself in a position where his interest and duty conflict.'
>
> Lord Herschell in *Bray* v. *Ford* [1896]

However, this has been called 'rather a counsel of prudence than a rule of equity'.

FURTHER THINKING

In *Motivex Ltd* v. *Bulfield* [1988] Vinelott J observed that: 'I do not think that it is strictly accurate to say that a director owes a fiduciary duty to the company not to put himself in a position where his duty to the company may conflict with his personal interest or with his duty to another.' Thus Lord Herschell's words should perhaps be rephrased to say that where there is a conflict between personal interests and duty as a trustee then the duty is not to take advantage of that conflict and to consider only the interests of the trust. See Koh (2003).

REVISION NOTE

Look again at Chapter 9 in the section on constructive trusts at cases where trustees have been held liable as constructive trustees as they have been in breach of their fiduciary duty. This is also a good example of where you can use the same cases to illustrate more than one point of law.

- The fiduciary nature of trusteeship prevents payment of trustees unless authorised by the trust instrument or by statute – the relevant one here is s.29, Trustee Act 2000.

- Trustees are also not allowed to purchase trust property but an exceptional case where they were is *Holder* v. *Holder* [1968].

Duties and powers of trustees

The fundamental duty of the trustee is the fiduciary duty (above) but there are specific duties and powers:

- A *duty* must be exercised, although the trustee has a discretion as to precisely how it is exercised (e.g. a trustee has a duty to invest but a discretion in what to invest in).
- A *power* is discretionary and so need not be exercised at all.

This is an area which is mainly governed by nineteenth century cases and is often considered to be in need of reform.

KEY CASE

***Re Beloved Wilkes' Charity* (1851) 3 Mac & G (HC)**

Concerning: whether trustees have to give reasons for their decisions

Facts

The trustees had a duty to select a boy to be educated for Holy Orders and had to give preference to boys from certain parishes. They selected a boy from another parish and did not give reasons for their decision.

Legal principle

The court will not compel trustees to give reasons for their decisions.

If the trustees do give reasons for their decisions then the court may investigate them but the precise grounds for doing so are not clear.

FURTHER THINKING

You need to think if the principle in this case is justifiable today and, if not, what should replace it. Trustees are not public bodies and so it may not be appropriate to impose the same duties on them to give reasons as applies, for example, to local authorities.

Relationship between powers in the trust instrument and statutory powers

The legislation on trustees' powers operates in default of any provision in the trust instrument to the contrary (see s.69(2), Trustee Act 1925). This is a useful point to explore in an essay question and is also relevant in problems (e.g. on powers of maintenance and advancement – see below).

Main duties of trustees

The duty to give information

The extent of the duty to give information to the beneficiaries is somewhat unclear and would form good material for an essay question on the extent to which trustees are accountable to the beneficiaries. There has been a shift from the approach in *Re Londonderry's Settlement* [1965], which emphasised that beneficiaries are allowed to see documents which contain information about the trust that the beneficiaries are entitled to know and in which the beneficiaries have a proprietary interest. In *Schmidt* v. *Rosewood Trust Ltd* (2003) the court emphasised that the issue is the requirement for the court to supervise the trust. .

Duty to act impartially

KEY CASE

***Howe* v. *Earl of Dartmouth* (1802) 7 Ves 137 Chan**

Concerning: duties of trustees between a life tenant and a remainderman

The facts of this case do not aid an understanding of the legal principle.

Legal principle

The trustee must act impartially and so must strike a balance between the interests of the life tenant (income required) and the remainderman (preservation of capital required).

Statutory duty of care

This was introduced by the Trustee Act 2000 and it is vital that you read the background to this Act. The fundamental reason why it was introduced was that the duties of trustees were governed mainly by nineteenth century case law which was quite out of date.

KEY STATUTE

Trustee Act 2000, s.1

A trustee shall exercise such care as is reasonable having regard in particular to:

(a) any special knowledge or experience which he has or holds himself out as having
(b) if he acts in the course of a business or profession, any special knowledge or experience which is reasonable to expect of person acting in that business or profession.

The statutory duty of care applies to:

- investment
- acquisition of land
- appointment of agents, etc.
- insurance
- compounding of liabilities
- reversionary interests, valuations and audit.

With regard to investment the following are relevant:

KEY STATUTE

Trustee Act 2000, s.3

A trustee may make any investment that he could make if he was absolutely entitled under the trust.

Trustee Act 2000, s.4

The standard investment criteria when investing are:

(a) the suitability to the trust of particular investments
(b) the need for diversification of investments, so far as this is appropriate.

Trustee Act 2000, s.5

A trustee must obtain and consider advice about the way in which the power of investment should be exercised. Note that s.5 defines what this is and when trustees are relieved of this duty.

Cases on investment may still be useful, even if decided under the previous law (e.g. *Cowan* v. *Scargill* [1985]).

Main powers of trustees

Powers of maintenance and advancement

KEY DEFINITION

Maintenance means payment of income to beneficiaries before they are entitled.

KEY DEFINITION

Advancement means payment of capital to beneficiaries before they are entitled.

These often come up in problem questions and Figure 11.1 shows a flow chart for answering them.

Figure 11.1

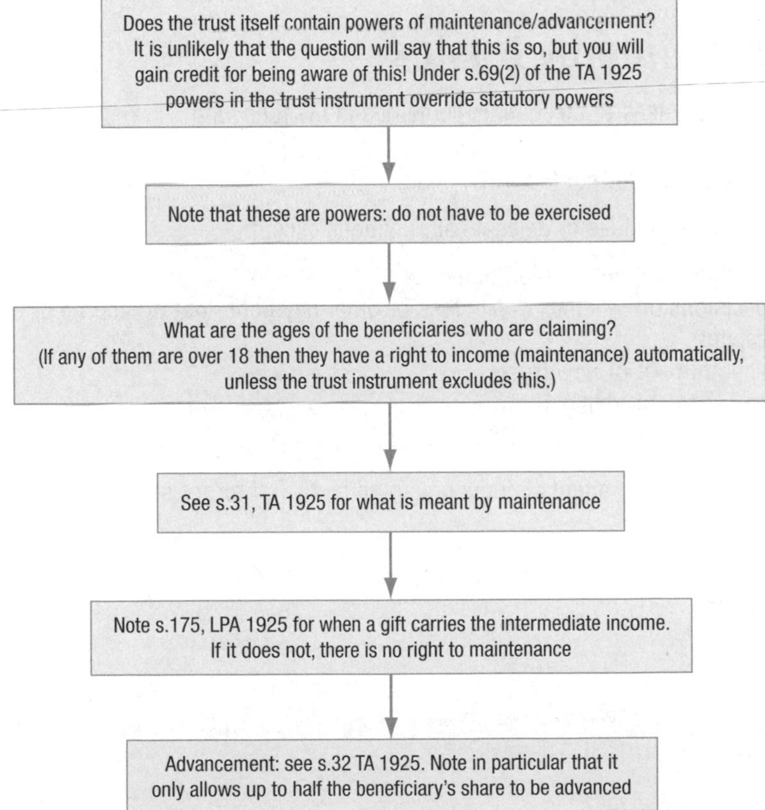

Does the trust itself contain powers of maintenance/advancement? It is unlikely that the question will say that this is so, but you will gain credit for being aware of this! Under s.69(2) of the TA 1925 powers in the trust instrument override statutory powers
Note that these are powers: do not have to be exercised
What are the ages of the beneficiaries who are claiming? (If any of them are over 18 then they have a right to income (maintenance) automatically, unless the trust instrument excludes this.)
See s.31, TA 1925 for what is meant by maintenance
Note s.175, LPA 1925 for when a gift carries the intermediate income. If it does not, there is no right to maintenance
Advancement: see s.32 TA 1925. Note in particular that it only allows up to half the beneficiary's share to be advanced

KEY CASE

***Re Kershaw's Trusts* (1868) LR 6 Eq 322 (HC)**

Concerning: meaning of advancement

Facts

An **advancement** was sought to enable the beneficiary's husband to set up in business and so prevent the family separating.

Legal principle

An advancement would be made. The term advancement has a wider meaning than just financial benefit.

Power to buy land

This is contained in s.8, TA 2000 and gives trustees very wide powers to buy land.

Delegation by trustees

The power of trustees to delegate is contained in the following:

KEY STATUTE

Trustee Act 2000, s.11

This allows trustees to delegate all functions except:

- decisions on distribution of assets
- decisions on whether to pay fees or other payments out of income or capital
- appointment of new trustees
- power to sub-delegate.

Liability for the acts of agents is now governed by the statutory duty of care in s.1, TA 2000 (above).

Exclusion of trustees' liability

KEY CASE

***Armitage* v. *Nurse* [1998] Ch 221 (HC)**

Concerning: extent to which trustees can exclude liability

Facts

The trust excluded the liability of the trustees for loss or damage unless caused by the actual fraud of the trustees.

Legal principle

This was upheld.

FURTHER THINKING

There is a view that trustee exclusion clauses have gone too far (e.g. see. McCormack (1998) and *Citibank NA* v. *MIBA Assurance SA* (2006).

In *Australian Securities and Investments Commission* v. *Citigroup Global Markets Australia Pty Ltd* (2007) an investment bank which advised on a takeover bid stipulated that it was not retained as a fiduciary. This was held to eliminate any liability by the bank when it traded in the shares of the company which its client proposed to take over. The case is also interesting as Jacobsen J distinguished between fiduciaries *per se* (i.e. of the kind this book has been discussing) and where there is a fiduciary relationship arising out of a specific relationship, as here (see Getzler (2008)).

Chapter summary: **Putting it all together**

TEST YOURSELF

- [ ] Can you tick all the points from the **revision checklist** at the beginning of this chapter?
- [ ] Take the **end-of-chapter quiz** on the companion website.
- [ ] Test your knowledge of the legal principles of the key cases and statutory provisions with the **revision flashcards** on the website.
- [ ] Attempt the **problem question** from the beginning of this chapter using the guidelines below.
- [ ] Go to the companion website and try out **other questions**.

Answer guidelines

See the problem question at the start of this chapter.

(a) Begin with s.1, TA 2000 (duty of care) and consider this in the light of s.3 (general powers of investment) and s.4 (criteria when investing). Trustees can take advice from others (see s.11, TA 2000) but is this a wise decision here? Note also that Kate is a beneficiary. See Personal Liability of Beneficiary, page 174.

(b) Possible conflict of interest, *Boardman* v. *Phipps* (1967). Steve may be liable for director's fees as a constructive trustee.

(c) Section 32, TA 1925 (power of advancement) – but it is not her money yet! Is she asking for too much? She is entitled to one third of £500,000 and only half of this can be advanced.

(d) Section 31, TA 1925 (power of maintenance) – does the gift carry the intermediate income? Even so, is this a proper case for maintenance? Trustees are committed to paying sums for years to come.

Make your answer stand out

You must know and apply the basic statute law accurately to gain a reasonable mark but for a really good mark you should do some research in the case law, especially on powers of advancement.

FURTHER READING

Dunn, A. (2001) 'Trusting in the Prudent Woman of Business' in *Feminist Perspectives on Equity and Trusts*, edited by S. Scott-Hunt and H. Lim, London: Cavendish Press.

Getzler, J. (2008) 'Excluding Fiduciary Duties: The Problem of Investment Banks', LQR 15.

Koh, J. (2003) 'Once a Director, Always a Fiduciary?', 62 CLJ 403.

McCormack, C. (1998) 'The Liabilities of Trustees for Gross Negligence', Conv. 100.

12 Variation of trusts

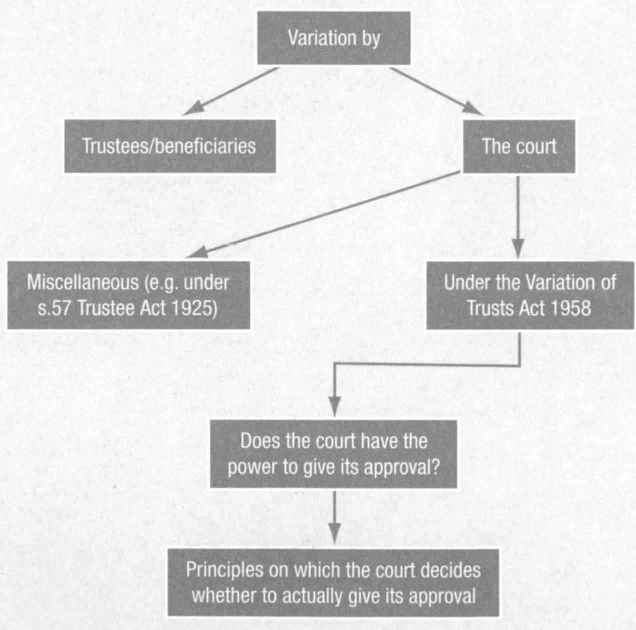

A printable version of this topic map is available from www.pearsoned.co.uk/lawexpress

Revision Checklist

Essential points you should know:

- [ ] how a trust can be varied
- [ ] the reasons why the Variation of Trusts Act 1958 (VTA) was passed
- [ ] the beneficiaries who can apply under the VTA
- [ ] the principles on which the court can approve variations under the VTA
- [ ] who the parties are to an application.

Introduction:
Understanding variation of trusts

This is not a difficult area and any question will almost certainly will not be linked to other areas, with the exception of one small point on formalities.

The focus of a question will be on the Variation of Trusts Act 1958 (VTA) although an essay question may involve other areas too. The VTA is relatively straightforward except for para. (b) of s.1(1), which, however, rarely appears in problem questions.

Assessment advice

Essay questions

A good answer will put this topic in its context rather then simply explaining the provisions of the VTA. In any essay question you need to be aware of the reasons why the VTA was passed, the limitations on its use and be able to discuss if the courts have gone beyond their powers in approving variations. You also need to consider the extent to which the views of the settlor/testator can be given weight. Select three or four cases and analyse them from the point of view of the interests of the beneficiaries (there may be conflicting interests here) and the wishes of the settlor/testator. Who came out top? Was this right? Another possibility is a general essay question on the whole topic of variation of trusts and here you will gain marks by being able to look at this topic in a broader context.

Assessment advice

Problem questions

Problem questions will focus on the VTA and above all you need a clear structure to your answer:

- Does the VTA apply?
- If so, should the court approve the variation sought? Note that the VTA requires that it should be for the benefit of the beneficiaries (except where the application is under para. (d) of s.1(1)). How has this been interpreted by the courts?
- Mention that the purpose of the VTA is to vary but not to resettle. What does this mean in the context of the problem?
- Who should the parties be?

Sample question

Could you answer this question? Below is a typical problem question that could arise on this topic. Guidelines on answering the question are included at the end of this chapter, whilst a sample essay question and guidance on tackling it can be found on the companion website.

Problem question

In 1998, under the will of John, his wife Julia became the life tenant of a fund of £750,000 with remainder to such of their children who attained the age of 21. There are three children, Peter (now 17), James (16) and Henry (14). Julia is now aged 54 and the fund stands at £1,500,000.

Julia wishes to reduce the amount of tax that she is paying on her income from the fund and so she wishes to reduce her interest in the fund to 25 per cent and divide the rest equally among her three children. However, she feels that 21 is too young an age for them to acquire such wealth especially as she regards Henry in particular as immature, and so she wishes the age at which they acquire their shares to be varied to 30.

In addition she wishes to live in France as she has acquired substantial business interests there although she may wish at a later date to relocate to Belgium. For now she wishes the trust to be administered from France.

Is the trust likely to be varied as Julia wishes?

Situations where a trust can be varied

Variation of trusts broadly means when a trustee or beneficiary wants to change the terms of the trust. Exams will focus mainly on how a trust can be varied under the VTA which gives the courts a *general* power to vary trusts, but you need to be aware of other situations where a trust can be varied to add depth to your answer.

Variation by trustees and beneficiaries

- Trustees under the trust instrument – this is unlikely to figure in the exam in detail.
- Beneficiaries under the Rule in *Saunders* v. *Vautier* (1841). This usually amounts to termination of the whole trust.

KEY CASE

***Saunders* v. *Vautier* (1841) Cr & Ph 240 (CA)**

Concerning: variation of trusts by the beneficiaries

The facts of this case do not aid an understanding of the legal principle.

Legal principle

If all the beneficiaries are of full age and *sui juris* (i.e. of full capacity) and are absolutely entitled to the trust property they can terminate the trust and demand that the fund is handed over to them.

Variation by the court

- **Miscellaneous powers.** S.57, Trustee Act 1925 – this allows the court to confer extra powers in the management and administration of the trust. A good instance is wider investment powers, although now that these have been increased (see s.3, Trustee Act 2000 in Chapter 11) this will not be needed so often.
- **Emergency powers** come under the inherent jurisdiction of the court: one example is where emergency action is needed to save a building from collapse.

You must point out that the above powers do not help where the parties wish to vary the actual terms of the trust (e.g. to vary the actual beneficial interests). This is where the law needs discussing in detail.

Example one

Anne (49) has a life interest under a trust established by their uncle John with remainder to her two daughters Lucy (20) and Emma (17) at the age of 21. Anne has other income and so she wishes to surrender her life interest so that her daughters become entitled absolutely at the age of 25. She feels that 21 is too young an age for them to acquire great wealth.

Think first whether this variation could be allowed under the rules stated above. The answer is no: *Saunders* v. *Vautier* (1841) cannot apply as Emma is 17 and it is not a change in the administration of the trust so we cannot use s.57, TA 1925.

So your answer needs to go on to look at the VTA.

Variation of trusts under the VTA 1958

KEY STATUTE

The Variation of Trusts Act 1958 (VTA)

This statute gives the courts a general power to vary trusts, unlike the specific situations above.

EXAM TIP

In an essay question sketch in the background to the VTA. Explain that the previous law did not allow the court to sanction variations of this kind and refer to *Chapman* v. *Chapman* [1954].

Does the court have the power to give its approval?

When can the VTA be used?

- It only applies to applications to vary an existing *trust* – note *Allen* v. *Distillers Co. (Biochemicals) Ltd* [1974]: in an exam problem question there will probably be a trust to which the VTA applies but you will still gain credit for raising this point.
- Is the court allowed to give its *approval*? This is only in four cases which are on behalf of:
  - (a) Infants and those who by reason of mental incapacity are incapable of assenting.
  - (b) This is a complex category which is basically beneficiaries who may be unascertainable at present but who may become entitled in the future on the happening of a particular event. It thus applies to those who have only an expectation of being beneficiaries (e.g. a potential future spouse) – see *Knocker* v. *Youle* [1986]. It is unlikely to appear in a problem question but may do so in an essay.
  - (c) Persons unborn.
  - (d) Persons with a discretionary interest under a protective trust.

EXAM TIP

(a) and (c) are the two categories most likely to appear in the exam. The examiner will want you to discuss the cases below on whether the application might succeed and so at this stage almost certainly either (a) or (c) above will apply.

REVISION NOTE

Check the term **protective trust** in the glossary before you go on.

EXAM TIP

Note who are not included: adult beneficiaries who are capable of consenting. If any of these are present (even one) then they must give consent themselves.

Should the court give its approval?

KEY STATUTE

Variation of Trusts Act 1958, s.2.1(1)

'the court shall not approve an arrangement on behalf of any person unless the carrying out thereof would be for the benefit of that person'.

The vital word here is 'benefit'. Keep coming back to this issue: is the variation for the benefit of those on whose behalf approval is sought?

Principles on which the court decides whether to give its approval

KEY CASE

***Re Weston's Settlements* [1969] 1 Ch 233 (CA)**

Concerning: meaning of benefit under the VTA

Facts

Approval was sought to vary a trust so that it would be governed by Jersey law. The settlor and his sons, the beneficiaries, now lived in Jersey. The motive for the variation was tax saving.

Legal principle

Financial benefit was not the only benefit to be considered. It was not for the benefit of the children to be uprooted from England just to save tax.

KEY CASE

***Re CL* [1969] 1 Ch 587 Court of Protection**

Concerning: benefit may be taking away one beneficiary's interest entirely

Facts

Approval was sought to the surrender of a protected life interest and an interest in remainder held by a mental patient so that it went to her daughter.

Legal principle

Approval would be given as the beneficiary was amply provided for and it was what she would have wished had she been able to give an opinion.

KEY CASE

***Re Remnant's Settlement Trusts* [1970] Ch 560 (HC)**

Concerning: avoidance of family trouble may be a reason for approving a variation

Facts

Approval was sought to vary a trust by deleting a clause where the children of two sisters forfeited their beneficial interests if they married a Roman Catholic or practised Roman Catholicism.

Legal principle

Approval would be given as the clause was a source of family dissension.

KEY CASE

***Re Holt's Settlement* [1969] 1 Ch 100 (HC)**

Concerning: variation which postponed the age at which an interest vested

Facts

Approval was sought to vary the age at which the interest of beneficiaries vested from 21 to 30. This was part of a larger scheme under which their mother would surrender one half of her life interest to them, the motive being tax saving.

Legal principle

This would be approved. Children 'should be reasonably advanced in a career and settled in life before they are in receipt of an income sufficient to make them independent of the need to work' (Megarry J).

EXAM TIP

The settlor's views: exam questions often ask you about this, especially essays. You should point out that, by reference to some of the above cases, the views of the settlor are certainly not decisive and may be ignored (e.g. *Re Remnant* [1970]. In *Re Weston* [1969] it was the settlor who actually applied for the variation. Read also *Re Steed's Will Trusts* [1960].

FURTHER THINKING

Less has been written on this area than on some others and so if you are able to show acquaintance with critical thought this will be an added bonus. Look at Cottrell (1971) and Luxton (1997).

Some last points to round off an answer:

- *Re Ball's Settlement* [1968] – the limits of the power to vary a trust: 'If an arrangement changes the whole substratum of a trust, then it may well be that it cannot be regarded merely as varying the trust' (Megarry J).
- Parties to an application: the settlor (if living) and all beneficiaries should be parties.

FURTHER THINKING

The effect of the variation will mean that the equitable interests of some beneficiaries will pass to others but what of s.53(1)(c), LPA 1925? How is it satisfied? A difficult point which students often miss. Do not be one of them but read what your textbook says!

REVISION NOTE

If you are not sure of what s.53(1)(c) is about check Chapter 5 now.

Chapter summary: **Putting it all together**

TEST YOURSELF

- [ ] Can you tick all the points from the **revision checklist** at the beginning of this chapter?
- [ ] Take the **end-of-chapter quiz** on the companion website.
- [ ] Test your knowledge of the legal principles of the key cases and statutory provisions with the **revision flashcards** on the website.
- [ ] Attempt the **problem question** from the beginning of the chapter using the guidelines below.
- [ ] Go to the companion website to try out **other questions**.

Answer guidelines

See the problem question at the start of this chapter.

This is not a difficult problem question but it is one where you must structure your answer very carefully. There are two separate situations and in each of them you need to consider (in this order):

1 Why it is necessary to apply the VTA.
2 Whether you think that the court should actually give its approval to the variation.

Now look at each situation:

- Change in age of vesting and Julia's proposal to increase the children's shares. Apply the VTA: can the court consent? Yes it can because the beneficiaries are infants (category (a)). Should it consent? Look at *Re Holt* [1969]. Probably will be approved but note that court must also look at the interests of any unborn children.
- Move to France: Again note that the VTA allows the court to approve but should it? Look at *Re Weston's Settlements* [1969] and note that here there is a possible later move to France. Unlikely to be approved.

In each case mention who the parties to the application should be.

Make your answer stand out

This is not an area where there has been as much academic discussion as in others and so extra points are less easy to find and, when found, are an added bonus. Mention the point above about the possible applicability of s.53(1)(c) LPA 1925.

FURTHER READING

Cottrell, R. (1971) 'Re Remnant's Settlement Trusts', 34 MLR 98.
Luxton, P. (1997) 'Variations of Trusts: Settlor's Intentions and the Consent Principle in Saunders v. Vautier', 60 MLR 719.

13 Breach of trust

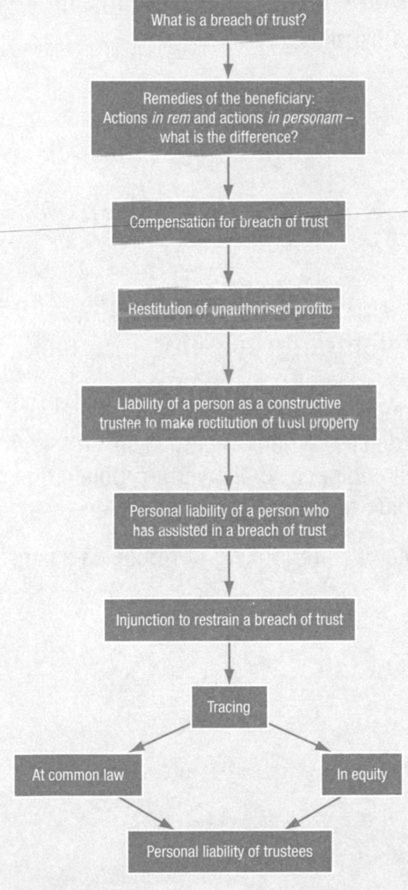

A printable version of this topic map is available from www.pearsoned.co.uk/lawexpress

Revision Checklist

Essential points you should know:

- [ ] when a breach of trust can arise
- [ ] the distinction between actions *in rem* and actions *in personam*
- [ ] the different principles on which compensation is awarded for breach of trust: significance of *Target Holdings* v. *Redfern (a firm)* [1996]
- [ ] when a person who has received trust property in breach of trust can be liable to the beneficiaries
- [ ] when a person who has assisted in a breach of trust (as distinct from receiving trust property) can be liable to the beneficiaries
- [ ] how to apply the rules governing the tracing of trust property
- [ ] the personal liability of trustees.

Introduction:
Understanding breach of trust

This is a complex area and needs careful study. The key is understanding how the different remedies interlock.

First learn the basic rules, concentrating on what each remedy is trying to achieve, and completely ignoring the details. When you are clear on this, move on! This way you will find that you are well equipped to answer a problem question and you can then progress to further reading to enable you to tackle an essay question.

Important note: In this chapter we are looking at remedies against either the trustees or the trust property.

Assessment advice

Essay questions

An essay question is likely to focus on the remedies available for a breach of trust. These are the following possibilities:

- a general question, as above
- one on compensation, where you will need a good knowledge of recent case law, in particular *Target Holdings* v. *Redferns (a firm)* [1996]
- a detailed look at tracing remedies: here you may be asked to compare tracing in equity with that at common law or, as below, you may be just asked to look at tracing in equity.

Problem questions

A likely question is a detailed one on following trust property where there has been a breach of trust. An example is set out below. Provided you take a logical approach you can earn very good marks here as there is usually a right or wrong answer to most points with some areas having room for discussion so that really good students can earn extra marks. An area to concentrate on when revising!

Sample question

Can you answer this question? Below is a typical problem question that could arise on this topic. Guidelines on answering the question are included at the end of the chapter whilst a sample essay question and guidance on tackling it can be found on the companion website.

Problem question

Joanna is a trustee of a fund set up by Anne for the benefit of her daughter, Sally. In 2001 Joanna transferred £20,000 from the trust account into her own personal account which, before the transfer, stood at £10,000. She then paid into her personal account the sum of £15,000 which she held as trustee under the will of her friend Dave.

In 2002 she withdrew £12,000 from her account to buy a racehorse but the horse had to be put down when it fell in a race. In 2003 she withdrew a further £6000 which she spent on tickets in a prize draw. She won first prize of £1000. In 2004 she withdrew £25,000 which she spent on a vintage car. In 2005 Joanna withdrew to a monastery in Tibet. She wrote to both Sally and Dave enclosing a cheque for £1000 for each of them and expressing remorse at what she had done. She donated all the rest of the money to the monastery. Joanna gave the car, which is now valued at £7000, to her daughter Millie.

Joanna has now been declared bankrupt.

Advise her trustee in bankruptcy and the beneficiaries under both trusts as to what remedies are available to them to restore the property to the trust.

What is a breach of trust?

Trustees are in breach of trust if they fail to observe the duties laid on them by equity and by the trust instrument.

REVISION NOTE

Go back to Chapter 11 and check that you are familiar with the duties of trustees.

Breaches may be:

- Fraudulent (e.g. wrongly taking trust property). *Attorney-General for Hong Kong* v. *Reid* [1994] (see Chapter 9) is a good example of fraud.
- Negligent (e.g. failing to review investments at proper intervals).

EXAM TIP

Begin your answer to a problem question on remedies by identifying the actual breach of trust which has occurred. Hardly any student does but this is the most important issue: no breach, no remedy, end of question! Of course there will be a breach but find it!

Remedies of the beneficiary

Actions *in rem* and actions *in personam*

An action *in personam* may be brought against the trustee for damages for breach of trust, but an action *in rem* may be brought to recover the trust property.

Example one: Action *in personam*

A trustee has a duty to invest the trust property and in this case invests all of the £5m trust fund in a small company on the advice of an inexperienced financial adviser. In fact all of the money is lost when the company goes into liquidation. The beneficiaries are entitled to a remedy but the position is not straightforward as they may not be entitled to all of the money back. It may be that there was a reason for investing some of the money in that company, but not all of it, or it may be that, on the facts, there was no liability at all as the advice was not negligent. Whatever the outcome, the point is that the remedy is for money compensation and is against the trustee personally (*in personam*).

Example two: Action *in rem*

A trustee of money in a bank account in the name of the trust wrongfully withdraws that money and puts it in his own bank account. The beneficiaries have a straightforward remedy: the return of the money. This is a remedy *in rem*, i.e. against the thing itself: in this example, the restitution of the money.

Types of remedies

These are as follows:

(a) compensation for breach of trust, as in Example one
(b) restitution of unauthorised profits
(c) personal liability as a constructive trustee to make restitution of trust property
(d) liability of a person who has assisted in a breach of trust
(e) an injunction to restrain a breach of trust
(f) liability to account as a constructive trustee where there is a right to trace trust property into that person's hands, as in Example two.

It may help to look at the remedies diagrammatically. In Figure 13.1 the letters refer to the list above:

Figure 13.1

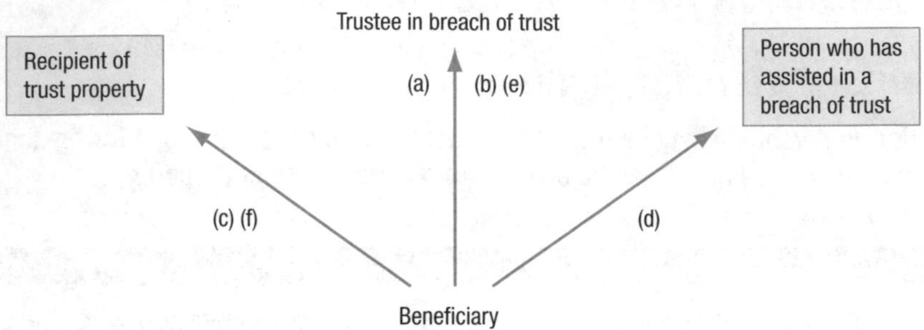

Note: the letters refer to the remedies above.

Figure 13.1 is deliberately called a snapshot: this topic is complex as it involves a number of different remedies and so at this stage it is only possible to give a general idea of where the remedies fit in. However, it is vital to start in this way.

EXAM TIP

When you are faced with a problem question on remedies draw a diagram like Figure 13.1 so that you are absolutely clear where the different remedies sought in the question fit in.

We will now look at each of the remedies in turn.

(a) Compensation for breach of trust

This remedy is appropriate where there has been, for example, negligence in the exercise of a duty under the trust, such as a duty to invest.

KEY CASE

***Target Holdings Ltd* v. *Redferns (a firm)* [1996] 1 AC 421 (HL)**

Concerning: principles to be applied when assessing compensation for breach of trust

Facts

X, solicitors, were acting for a mortgagor (borrower) and a mortgagee (lender) and received a mortgage advance on trust to release it to the mortgagor when the transfers of properties were executed. However, in breach of trust they released it early, on the day before contracts were exchanged, and the mortgagee subsequently lost money as the value of the properties had been overstated. The mortgagee claimed against the solicitors for this loss.

Legal principle

In assessing compensation for breach of trust in commercial dealings such as this, bearing in mind that the solicitor was only a bare trustee, a trustee is only liable for losses caused by the breach and not for losses which would have occurred in any event. The mortgage would have gone through anyway, and so the fact that the solicitors had released the mortgage advance early did not cause the loss.

(b) Restitution of unauthorised profits

This remedy is appropriate where there has been a breach of a fiduciary duty by making an unauthorised profit.

REVISION NOTE

Go back to Chapter 9 and check that you know the cases (e.g. *Boardman* v. *Phipps* [1967]) on fiduciary duties and their breach.

In *Tang Man Sit* v. *Capacious Investments Ltd* [1996] the remedies of compensation and restitution were both possible and the claimant had to choose between them.

(c) Personal liability as a constructive trustee to make restitution of trust property

These are often called knowing receipt cases.

Example three

John is trustee of a small charity. The charity owns a mini-bus and John sells this, in breach of trust, to Jack. The charity wish to take action.

The charity could claim against John under (b) above to make restitution of the money he has received. In addition it could claim against Jack if Jack is a constructive trustee. Will he be? Jack may say that he had no idea that the mini-bus belonged to the charity.

Problem area: Test for liability

There two current views:

1. Lord Millet in *Twinsectra* v. *Yardley* (2002): 'Liability for knowing receipt is receipt based. It does not depend on fault.' The essence of this approach is that it imposes strict liability.
2. Nourse LJ in *Bank of Credit and Commerce International (Overseas Ltd)* v. *Akindele* [2001]: 'The recipient's state of knowledge must be such as to make it unconscionable for him to retain the benefit of the receipt.' The essence of this approach is that it does involve fault.

The literature on this topic is vast but you could start with Ellinger (2005).

See also *Farah Constructions Pty Ltd and others* v. *Say-Dee Pty Ltd* (2007) where the High Court of Australia held that liability for receipt of trust property is not based on a general principle of unjust enrichment and rejected the notion that liability was strict and not fault based.

If a person is a volunteer (i.e. has received trust property as a gift) then they must always restore the property.

REVISION NOTE

Remember the maxim: Equity will not assist a volunteer – Chapter 6.

FURTHER THINKING

This decision is of great importance and the divergent approaches of the Australian courts are a perfect example of the debate which will always exist in equity. See the excellent analysis of the Court of Appeal's decision by Nolan and Conaglen (2007).

(d) Liability of a person who has assisted in a breach of trust

Example four

Take Example three above. Suppose that when John wanted to sell the mini-bus he asked Steve, a friend, to find a buyer and it was through Steve that Jack bought it.

Here it is wrong to talk of a person like Steve as a constructive trustee as he has not received trust property but he can be made liable in equity.

Lord Hutton in *Twinsectra* v. *Yardley* (2002):

> 'The person must be dishonest and this means that his conduct must be dishonest by the ordinary standards of reasonable and honest people and he realised that by those standards his conduct was dishonest.'

However, in *Barlow Clowes International (in liquidation)* v. *Eurotrust International Ltd* (2006), the Judicial Committee of the Privy Council held that in cases of dishonest assistance in a breach of trust a person is dishonest if they had knowledge of the elements of the transaction which rendered their participation contrary to the ordinary standards of honest behaviour. The question is whether this has changed the law from what it was thought to be after the decision of the House of Lords in *Twinsectra* v. *Yardley*.

(e) Injunction to restrain a breach of trust

REVISION NOTE

Injunctions are dealt with in Chapter 2.

Example five

Suppose that the beneficiaries in example four had learned in advance of John's plans to sell the mini-bus. They could have restrained him from doing this by an injunction.

(f) Tracing

KEY DEFINITION

The term **tracing**, as with restitution, is often misunderstood. It is not a remedy as such but a right to trace (i.e. follow) trust property into the hands of a person who then becomes a constructive trustee of it.

Example six

Jane is trustee of the funds at her local tennis club. She takes out £5000 from the funds and uses the money to buy a car. Can the tennis club trace its funds to her car so that the car becomes trust property and, if it wishes, could the club sell it?

Tracing at common law

This right is limited and it does not allow **tracing** in one of the most common cases: where the defendant has mixed the trust's money in his own bank account and then gone bankrupt.

Tracing in equity

Keep two distinct points in mind:

1 Is tracing possible?
2 If so, can it be done?

First, there are four conditions as to whether tracing is possible:

1 Existence of a fiduciary relationship.

FURTHER THINKING

The necessity for this has been criticised. Lord Millett in *Foskett* v. *McKeown* [2001] said that there was no logical justification for it.

2 Existence of an equitable proprietary interest (e.g. that of a beneficiary).
3 Tracing would not be inequitable: see *Re Diplock* [1948].
4 Property must be in a traceable form. This means that the property must be ascertainable and this will not be so if, for example, it has been spent on a holiday.

KEY CASE

***Bishopsgate Investment Management (in liquidation)* v. *Homan* [1995] Ch 211 (CA)**

Concerning: loss of the right to trace

The facts of this case do not aid an understanding of the legal principle.

Legal principle

Tracing will not be permitted into an overdrawn account as clearly the property into which it is sought to trace has disappeared.

Second, we turn to consider whether tracing can be done.

Follow through these rules. They are ones most likely to arise in an exam.

EXAM TIP

Problem questions will almost certainly concentrate on the position where a trustee has mixed trust money with his own.

RULE ONE

KEY CASE

Re Hallett's Estate (1880) 13 Ch D (HC)

Concerning: withdrawals from an account

Legal principle

When making withdrawals from an account a trustee is presumed to spend his own money first. Once the amount in the account falls below the amount of trust funds then it is assumed that part of the trust funds must have been spent. Any later payments into the account are not treated as repayments of the trust money unless the trustee has shown an intention to do this (*Roscoe (James) (Bolton)* v. *Winder* [1915]).

Example seven

A trustee (X) puts £10,000 of trust money and £3000 of his own money into the trust account. He takes out £11,000 and spends it. £3000 of this is presumed to be his own money, but the remainder must be trust money. Therefore there is now £2000 of trust money left. He then puts £3000 into the account. This is presumed to be his own money unless X shows an intention to repay the trust money. If he does not then although the beneficiaries can claim the £2000 in the account they will have to take their place along with X's other creditors in a claim for the balance.

RULE TWO

In *Re Oatway* [1903] it was held that if a trustee mixes his own and trust money in an account and then takes all the money and spends it on identifiable property the beneficiaries have a first charge on this property for the recovery of the trust money.

KEY CASE

Foskett v. _McKeown_ [2001] 1 AC 102 (HL)

Concerning: position where the trust fund has increased in value

Legal principle

Lord Millett held that the beneficiary may claim either:

(a) a share in the fund in proportion to which the original trust fund bore to the mixed fund at the date when it was mixed, or
(b) they may have a lien on the fund to secure a personal claim against the fund for the return of the money (per Lord Millett).

Thus any increase in value can be claimed under option (a) but if the fund has decreased in value, then the beneficiaries can have a lien under option (b) for the amount that they are owed.

RULE THREE

The position where mixed funds in an account represent the funds of two or more trusts or the funds of a trust and an innocent volunteer. We are concerned here with two types of competing claim:

1 between two or more persons with a right to trace
2 between a person with a right to trace and an innocent volunteer.

Rule in *Re Clayton* (1816)

The Rule in this case provides that in the case of an active continuing bank account the trustee is regarded as having taken out of the fund whatever had been first put in: basically, 'first in, first out'.

Example eight

X, a trustee, puts £1000 of trust A money into a bank account on 1 June and £500 of trust B money into the same account on 2 June. There is now a total of £1500 trust money in the account. X then takes out £1200, and, in breach of trust, spends this. As the trust A money was put in first he is presumed to have taken all of this out together with £200 of trust B money. The remaining £300 belongs to trust B.

In *Barlow Clowes International Ltd (in liquidation)* v. *Vaughan* [1992] the rule in *Re Clayton* (1816) – *Clayton's Case* – was not applied to claims by investors regarding share in the assets of a company which had managed investment plans for them. The exact date on which sums owing to individuals were paid in could have simply been by chance (e.g. delay in delivery of their letter with the money).

Personal liability of trustees

EXAM TIP

The main focus of exam questions here will be on the extent to which trustees can escape liability: note carefully s.61 and s.62 of the Trustee Act 1925 and also the general equitable principle

A beneficiary who is of full age and capacity and who is in possession of all the relevant facts and who freely consents to a breach of trust cannot sue in respect of it afterwards.

Chapter summary: **Putting it all together**

TEST YOURSELF

- ☐ Can you tick all the points from the **revision checklist** at the beginning of this chapter?
- ☐ Take the **end-of-chapter quiz** on the companion website.
- ☐ Test your knowledge of the cases with the **revision flashcards** on the website.
- ☐ Attempt the **problem question** from the beginning of this chapter using the guidelines below.
- ☐ Go to the companion website and try out **other questions**.

Answer guidelines

See the problem question at the start of the chapter.

Joanna is a trustee and has committed breaches of trust. Therefore equitable remedies are available against her. Of these, the personal remedies are of no use as she is bankrupt and so has no assets. So we must turn to remedies against the trust property – proprietary remedies and, in particular, tracing. Go through the conditions which must be satisfied for tracing remedy to exist – there is an equitable proprietary interest but two conditions may not be satisfied in each case: tracing must not be inequitable and the property must be in traceable form. If a condition does not exist then there is no point in considering tracing further.

Follow through the sequence of events:

1. Joanna deposits £20,000 from the first trust account (we will refer to this as Trust A) into her own account. Her account then stands at £30,000.
2. She then pays in £15,000 from Trust B. Her account now stands at £45,000.
3. She withdraws £12,000 from her account to buy a racehorse. This must come first from her own money (*Re Hallett's Estate* (1880)) which is now spent and then probably from Trust A money (*Clayton's Case* (1816) but note here *Barlow Clowes International Ltd* v. *Vaughan* (1992)). As the racehorse is dead the money is no longer traceable. So there is now £33,000 left in the account made up of:
   - £18,000 Trust A money (£20,000 less £2000 spent in breach of trust)
   - £15,000 Trust B money.
4. Withdrawal of £6000 to buy tickets: from Trust A. The prize of £1000 may be claimed by Trust A (*Re Oatway* [1903], this sum has not been included in the final calculation, *Re Tilley's Will Trust* [1967] and *Foskett* v. *McKeown* [2001]). There is now £27,000 of which £12,000 is left.

5 Withdrawal of £25,000 to buy a car: this must be first from Trust A (£12,000). Trust A is now exhausted. And then £13,000 from Trust B. Now £2000 is left of Trust B's money.
6 Loss of £18,000 on the car: Trusts A and B will share rateably in any losses.
7 Money to monastery: must come from Trust B – cannot be traced? Is tracing inequitable? *Re Diplock* [1948].
8 Letter: appears to be repayment – *Roscoe* v. *Winder* [1915].

Make your answer stand out

Many students omit the material in the introductory paragraph. This is vital. Do include it!

FURTHER READING

Gardner, (2003) *An Introduction to the Law of Trusts*, 2nd edn, Oxford: Oxford University Press, pp. 265–85.

Nolan, R. and Conaglen, M. (2007) 'Strict Liability for Receipt of Misapplied Trust Property – Confusion Abounds', at 66 CLJ 19.

And finally, before the exam . . . .

TEST YOURSELF

- ☐ Look at the revision checklists at the start of each chapter. Are you happy that you can now tick them all? If not, go back to the particular chapter and work through the material again. If you are still struggling, **seek help** from your tutor.
- ☐ Go to the companion website and revisit the interactive **quizzes** provided for each chapter.
- ☐ Make sure you can recall the **legal principles** of the key cases and statutes which you have revised.
- ☐ Go to the companion website and test your knowledge of cases and terms with the **revision flashcards.**
- ☐ Go through each case in the text and make sure that you know the legal principle of each. You may find it helpful to make a separate list of these cases, write down the name of each and under it leave space for you to write in the legal principle. Do the same for statutes. Concentrate on the legal principle and remember to use the facts to illustrate the principle.
- ☐ Do the same for all the key definitions.
- ☐ Identify some of the key concepts of equity: a good start would be notice, discretion in the award of remedies, fiduciaries and unconscionability. Make sure that you can discuss them as concepts rather then just using them as terms.
- ☐ Check through all areas where there is an overlap between topics because this will help you in revising. This is dealt with below.

Linking it all up

Check where there are overlaps between subject areas. Make a careful note of these as a knowledge of how one topic can lead into another can increase your marks significantly. Here are some examples:

- **Constructive trusts**. A question on the nature of equity, nature of trusts, trustees, the fiduciary relationship, trusts of the home and of course a question on this topic itself.
- **Trustees**. A question on constructive trusts, the fiduciary relationship and a question on this topic itself.
- **Three certainties**. A question on secret trusts, formalities, constitution and one on three certainties itself.
- **Non-charitable purpose trusts**. A question on the nature of trusts, charitable trusts (problem questions often ask you about situations involving both charitable and non-charitable trusts), nature of equity and this topic itself.
- **Equitable maxims**. Essay questions on the maxims are excellent vehicles for bringing together knowledge on various topics: e.g. equity does not allow a statute to be used as an instrument of fraud: secret trusts, constructive trusts. Equity looks to the intent and not the form: secret trusts, constitution of trusts, certainty of intention. Equity does not assist a volunteer. Constitution of trusts. Nature of a trust.
- **Nature of equity**. This topic is such a good example and such a common exam question that a more detailed plan for bringing together different strands of the whole subject is set out below.

Essay question

'The function of the common law is to establish rules to govern the generality of cases . . . The function of equity is to restrain or restrict the exercise of legal rights and powers in particular cases, whenever it would be unconscionable for them to be exercised to the full.'

(Watt, *Trusts and Equity*, 2003).

Consider and illustrate this statement by reference to the nature and application of modern equity.

Answer guidelines

- The question asks about modern equity so no marks at all for history!
- Deal with the common law point: is it true to say that it is only concerned with generalities? Generally yes. For example, consideration in contract applies across the whole range of contracts, but with the duty of care in negligence there are variations. No need for much detail on common law but show you can contrast the two systems.
- Contrast equity and deal with the exact points raised.
- There are two of these:
  - (a) Does equity operate to restrict or restrain legal rights and responsibilities?
  - (b) Is the basis of its jurisdiction unconscionability?

In both cases it can be suggested that the statement oversimplifies:

(a) Equity is not just about seeking to prevent injustice occurring in the application of legal rules.
(b) Equitable jurisdiction is not just about restraining unconscionability.

Make your answer stand out
A clear analysis of terminology is needed. For instance, what is meant by 'unconscionability' and 'principle'.

Glossary

Key definitions

Advancement	Payment of capital to beneficiaries before they are entitled.
Bare trustee	A trustee with no active duties and so can be given directions by the beneficiary to transfer the legal estate.
Beneficiaries	Those for whom the property is held in trust.
Constitution of a trust	A trust is constituted when the legal title to the trust property is vested in the trustee(s).
Constructive trusts	Defined by Millett (Equity's Place in the Law of Commerce 1998 114 LQR 214) as arising 'whenever the circumstances are such that it would be unconscionable for the owner of the legal title to assert his own beneficial interest and deny the beneficial interest of another'.
Cy-près	So near (i.e. allows property to be used for charitable purposes so near to the original ones where these have failed).
Discretionary trust	Where the trustees have a discretion as to whether a person will be a beneficiary or not.
Estoppel	This arises when the representee has been led to act on the representation of the representor. If the representee then acts to their detriment on the basis of this promise, then in equity the court may grant them a remedy.
Fixed trusts	Where the interests in the trust property are fixed in the trust instrument.
Half-secret trusts	Where the will or other document discloses the existence of the trusts but not the details.
Injunction	An order requiring a party either to do or not to do a particular act.
Maintenance	Means payment of income to beneficiaries before they are entitled.
Marriage consideration	In equity includes the husband and wife and the issue of the marriage.
Misrepresentation	An untrue statement of fact which induces a person to enter into a transaction.
Notice	A purchaser is taken to have notice of an equitable interest unless they had either actual notice of the equitable interest of the beneficiaries, or constructive notice or imputed notice.

Protective trusts	Where there is a determinable life interest (determinable e.g. on the bankruptcy of the beneficiary) followed by a discretionary trust if the interest does determine.
Rescission	This remedy restores the parties to their position before the contract or other transaction was made.
Rectification	Where a written instrument (e.g. a contract) does not accord with the actual intentions of the parties it can be made to do so by an order of rectification.
Resulting trust	The beneficial interest results to, or jumps back to, the settlor who created the trust. The basis of an action founded on a resulting trust is therefore that one is seeking to recover one's own property.
Rule against perpetuities	Provides that a gift to be held for a non-charitable purpose trust is void if it may last beyond lives or lives in being plus 21 years.
Rule for certainty of objects in fixed trusts	All the beneficiaries must be capable of being listed, i.e. there must be no doubt as to who the beneficiaries are.
Rule for certainty of objects in discretionary trusts	Can it be said with certainty that any given individual is or is not a member of the class.
Secret trusts	Where the will or other document does disclose the existence of the trust.
Settlor	The settlor is in effect the creator of the trust which is created by the settlor transferring property to the trustees to hold on trust or alternatively declaring that they are the trustees. If the trust is created by will then the trust is created by the testator.
Specific performance (SP)	An order requiring the performance of obligations under a contract. Whereas injunctions are generally negative (you must not) SP is positive (you must).
Tracing	A right to trace (i.e. follow) trust property into the hands of a person who then becomes a constructive trustee of it.
Trust	'A trust is a relationship which arises when property is vested in (a person or) persons called the trustees, which those trustees are obliged to hold for the benefit of other persons called the *cestuis que trust* or beneficiaries' (Martin and Hanbury, *Modern Equity* 17th edn, p.47).
Unconstitution of a trust	A trust is unconstituted when the legal title to the trust property is not vested in the trustees.
Volunteer	A person who has not provided any consideration for a promise.

Index

Emboldened page references indicates that the entry appears in the glossary